Praise for
Rediscovering the
USS
ALLIGATOR

"Science, technology, and the human spirit merge in Dan Basta's new book documenting the search for the little-known Civil War-era USS Alligator submarine — one of the most intriguing inventions in America's naval history. A must-read for marine-exploration enthusiasts, educators, inventors, and history buffs."
Rear Admiral Jay Cohen, Former Head of the Office of Naval Research

"This is a classic tale of history forgotten and lost. The search for a pioneering submarine, that as yet remains unfound, revealed far more than was ever before known. Masterfully told, Dan Basta's recounting of the search for the Alligator is an instructive tale of how and why we should search for the past."
Dr. James P. Delgado, World-renowned Marine Archeologist

"We hear about incredible shipwrecks found at the bottom of the sea, but never the story of what it takes to mount the expeditions to find them. In this book, Basta tells the fascinating behind-the-scenes story of the search for the U.S. Navy's first submarine, lost in a storm in 1863. The story reveals how expeditions like this don't just happen. It takes historians, maritime archeologists, model builders, ship captains, oceanographers, and even documentary filmmakers. A book worth reading."
Steven Burns, World-renowned Documentary Filmmaker

Illustration of Alligator Model of
President Abraham Lincoln's "Secret Weapon."

Rediscovering the USS ALLIGATOR

THE U.S. NAVY'S "LOST" FIRST SUBMARINE

DANIEL J. BASTA

atmosphere press

© 2025 Daniel J. Basta

Published by Atmosphere Press

Cover design by Ronaldo Alves
On the cover: "The Launching 1 May 1862," a painting by Jim Christley

No part of this book may be reproduced without permission from the author except in brief quotations and in reviews.

Atmospherepress.com

Dedication

Michael Overfield
1955 – 2009

Mike Overfield, marine archeologist, doing what he loved most, in the control room of YP-679 on the Hunt for the USS *Alligator*.

Preface

This is a book I never intended to write. After all, a film on the subject, *Hunt for the U.S.S. Alligator: U.S. Navy's First Sub* had been released, numerous news stories published, abundant references posted on the internet, websites created, and even a nonprofit, *Friends of the Alligator*, established. I thought that everything had already been said and there wasn't much that I could add. What's more, the reality was that, after all the fanfare and excitement of our search for the lost submarine, we had failed to find the USS *Alligator*. But looking back gave me a different perspective, and talking with my old friend and co-conspirator, Jay Cohen, prompted me to think about writing this book. It was more than 20 years ago that Jay, then a rear admiral (RADM) in the U.S. Navy, and I first met in the South Pacific and were brought together by the story of the USS *Alligator*. I realized that no one had explained or connected all the dots in our search, including what actually had happened. No one had written much about the people involved and the decisions made behind the curtains. And so, I began to write this story. In the telling, I interchange USS *Alligator* and *Alligator* as seems to fit.

I also thought that writing the *Alligator* story as I remember it might be of interest to my colleagues and other participants in the events, even if they saw it differently from where they sat. But the more I thought about it, I also realized there are lessons here for others who dare to explore. Sometimes we learn more from events when they don't turn out as planned. Certainly, this was the case for our journey to rediscover and hunt for the *Alligator*. Lastly, the story of the *Alligator* deserves to stay alive and the USS *Alligator*'s place in U.S. naval history needs to be solidified. I hope this book helps do both. It is not a detailed history, but simply the story of the rediscovery and search to find the U.S. Navy's first submarine. It is a true story.

TABLE OF CONTENTS

Chapter 1	An Unlikely Journey	1
Chapter 2	The *Alligator*'s Place Among Early Submarines	7
Chapter 3	Serendipity in the South Pacific	13
Chapter 4	Like Minds Go to Work	20
Chapter 5	Paris Is a City of Light	36
Chapter 6	New Momentum	41
Chapter 7	A Film Changes Everything	53
Chapter 8	Expedition to Ocracoke	68
Chapter 9	The Hunt Continues	85
Chapter 10	Aftermath and Spinoffs	107
Epilogue		114
Appendices		118
Acknowledgements		139

Appendices

Appendix A: *Alligator* as Designed by De Villeroi
for the U.S. Navy 118

Appendix B: Submarine Propeller Designed by
De Villeroi for the French Navy 120

Appendix C: 1861 Contract Agreement to
Build the USS *Alligator* 122

Appendix D: Selected USS *Alligator* Correspondence 124

Appendix E: Derived Technical Description of the
USS *Alligator* 130

Appendix F: Correspondence Documenting Lincoln's
Visit to the USS *Alligator* 137

Chapter 1
An Unlikely Journey

This book tells the unlikely story of how the U.S. Navy's first submarine, the USS *Alligator*, was resurrected in the annals of U.S. naval history. Looking back, it's sometimes hard to believe that the events described here took place between May 2002, at the first whisper of an unknown submarine, and early 2007, when the Discovery Science Channel released *Hunt for the U.S.S. Alligator: U.S. Navy's First Sub*. The film provides an excellent account of the USS *Alligator* and our early efforts to find it. But how did the events surrounding the *Alligator*, including the film, come about? The story of this journey and its cast of participants has never been told. As I personally experienced many of the *Alligator* events, I hope this book enthusiastically shares the story — from the very beginning until the end of the tale.

A Mystery

USS *Alligator* was a secret weapon conceived during the early, dark days of the American Civil War. After a brief and clandestine career, she vanished from U.S. naval history. The USS *Alligator* was built at the same time and for the same purpose as the USS *Monitor*, an ironclad warship. The Monitor arrived at Hampton Roads first, and after the Battle with the CSS *Virginia* the USS *Monitor* went on to world fame and changed

Jim Christley's painting of the USS *Alligator* set adrift during the storm.

warship design forever. Just as John Ericsson, the creator of the *Monitor*, challenged conventional thinking, so did Brutus de Villeroi, the self-proclaimed French genius who designed the *Alligator*. The USS *Alligator* holds the honor as the first U.S. Navy submarine to be constructed and the first to be deployed on a combat mission[1]. Like the USS *Monitor*, it was a technological marvel of the time. Its construction and deployment pre-date the well-known Confederate submarine, the CSS *Hunley*, which possessed none of the *Alligator*'s innovations. In 1863, the *Alligator* was lost at sea in a storm off of Cape Hatteras while being towed south to operate against the Confederate defenses at Charleston and Savannah. The *Monitor* sank during a storm in the same waters the year before in 1862.

Unlike the well-known *Monitor*, the *Alligator*, which possessed such promise as a truly secret weapon, was known

---

1 See Appendices C and D.

only within a small circle of advisors, including U.S. President Abraham Lincoln[2]. When it disappeared at sea during the 1863 nor'easter, it essentially disappeared from history as well. Had the *Alligator* survived, the trajectory of submarine history may have been profoundly altered. Just as the USS *Monitor* irrevocably changed the design of modern warships, a successful deployment of the USS *Alligator* could have ushered in an era of submarine development and use in navies worldwide. It took nearly 40 years for the U.S. Navy to construct another submarine. By then, no one remembered the *Alligator*.

Nonetheless, rumors and whispers about the *Alligator* persisted, passing along information about a sophisticated U.S. Navy submarine early in the American Civil War. But its existence remained in the shadows for nearly 150 years until 2002, when a short article appeared in a Civil War magazine. As serendipity would have it, Nancy Cohen — the wife of Rear Admiral (RADM) Jay Cohen, then the head of the U.S. Navy's Office of Naval Research (ONR) — read it and was intrigued. This started a chain of unlikely events that led to the rediscovery and eventual search for the USS *Alligator* itself, and this is where our story begins.

Oddly, the story unfolds in the distant South Pacific and eventually involves a myriad of organizations and units, including the U.S. Navy, the National Oceanic and Atmospheric Administration (NOAA), the U.S. Naval Academy, academia, maritime museums in the U.S. and in France, interested individuals, descendants of original *Alligator* participants, and even filmmakers.

---

2 See Appendix F.

Early Detective Work

The story reveals the unexpected way in which history is sometimes re-discovered and brought back to life. It begins as a detective story, of sorts, that gains momentum inch by inch as more is learned and people are enlisted into the investigation. It illustrates how following various clues often leads to a point where the clues converge, and an overall investigation leapfrogs forward, even at times when it seems to have reached a dead end.

Individuals are portrayed conducting first-rate detective work, doggedly following the crumbs of history. As the quest took form, it was unclear as to who discovered whom first. Did the few enthusiasts working in the shadows, keeping the USS *Alligator* story alive, discover us when we began our search? Or did we discover them? In the end, it didn't matter. Common purpose simply drew everyone together. I think there is a lesson to learn from this. More than once, I have stolen the message from Hans Christian Andersen's fable about Stone Soup in which people collectively make a soup to feed a famine-plagued village. It explains how something can be accomplished when individuals come together to achieve something that no one can achieve alone. The rediscovery and hunt for the *Alligator* was truly the process of "making stone soup."

As individuals probed for information and followed leads, we discovered much about the USS *Alligator* and its inventor, Brutus de Villeroi. We encountered inevitable dead ends, and incredible luck lent a hand, revealing unexpected findings that eventually brought the USS *Alligator* back from the shadows. Perhaps the most well-known of these fortuitous events was the discovery of the original construction drawings for the USS *Alligator* in a cardboard box in Paris, France. It's a remarkable story that attracted filmmakers at the Discovery

Science Channel and pushed the project along at a higher pitch and into expeditions at sea that we had not really expected to undertake.

As the story unfolds researchers analyze and piece together fragments of information and undertake a metrological and oceanographic analyses to replicate the 1863 nor'easter weather conditions off of Cape Hatteras that led to the *Alligator's* loss. In the end, however, it is a complicated endeavor to determine where the *Alligator* may have come to rest on the sea floor. During the expeditions, many unknowns and the "Cape Hatteras Jinx" make finding the remains of the *Alligator* an extremely difficult proposition — and it remains so today.

Needle in a Haystack

Chapters chronicle the efforts to find the *Alligator* between 2004 and 2006 — some of the efforts not well known or not known at all — as intrepid scientists and researchers go to sea. In every attempt, the turbulent conditions off of Cape Hatteras intercede and frustrate the efforts. Even with relatively advanced underwater search technology, things go unexpectedly wrong. In the end, after more than four years, and to the disappointment of everyone involved, the remains of the USS *Alligator* have yet to be found. The submarine, or what's left of it, remains in the dangerous, swirling waters known as the "Graveyard of the Atlantic." She is a needle among needles in a haystack. The 47-foot *Alligator* lies somewhere on the sea bottom, in the company of many ships lost in the Graveyard. A time will come when someone else will take on the challenge and, once again, hunt for the USS

Alligator. Hopefully, the telling of this story will motivate the next searchers and make their quest a bit easier!

In the final chapter, I explain some of the benefits — beyond anyone's expectations — that undertaking the search eventually provided. Sometimes this is where the real value resides in such endeavors. As said in the Discovery film *Hunt for the U.S.S. Alligator: U.S Navy's First Sub*, the USS *Alligator* may itself still be lost, but she has now been found. Finally and hopefully, this story is revealing, reasonably well told, and interesting, especially to those who would embark on their own quests of discovery.

Chapter 2

The *Alligator's* Place Among Early Submarines

It was by no means the only submarine, or so-called "infernal machine," proposed to the Union at the time of the American Civil War. But it was the only submarine that the Union built and deployed on a combat mission. At the time it was constructed, the *Alligator* was the latest in a long line of developments — spanning back well before the American Revolution — aimed at building a vessel that could operate beneath the waves.

People may have always been curious about working beneath the water's surface. In fact, efforts to do so may go back to ancient times. But it was the practical needs of harvesting from the sea, constructing, salvaging, and war that drove submarine development. The technology of submarines, as we know them today, including the *Alligator* and its contemporaries, emerged from the Industrial Revolution. During this period, the enormous leaps forward in metallurgy, science, physics, and engineering ushered in the submarines' relatively rapid evolution. In a little more than 100 years, the submarine went from a wooden, one-man, hand-propelled "barrel" that barely moved just below the surface — David Bushnell's 1776 *Turtle* — to the fully functional submarines that entered the Great War in 1914. Crafted in the middle of this period of rapid evolution, the 1862 *Alligator* was likely the most advanced submarine in the world, at least for a short time.

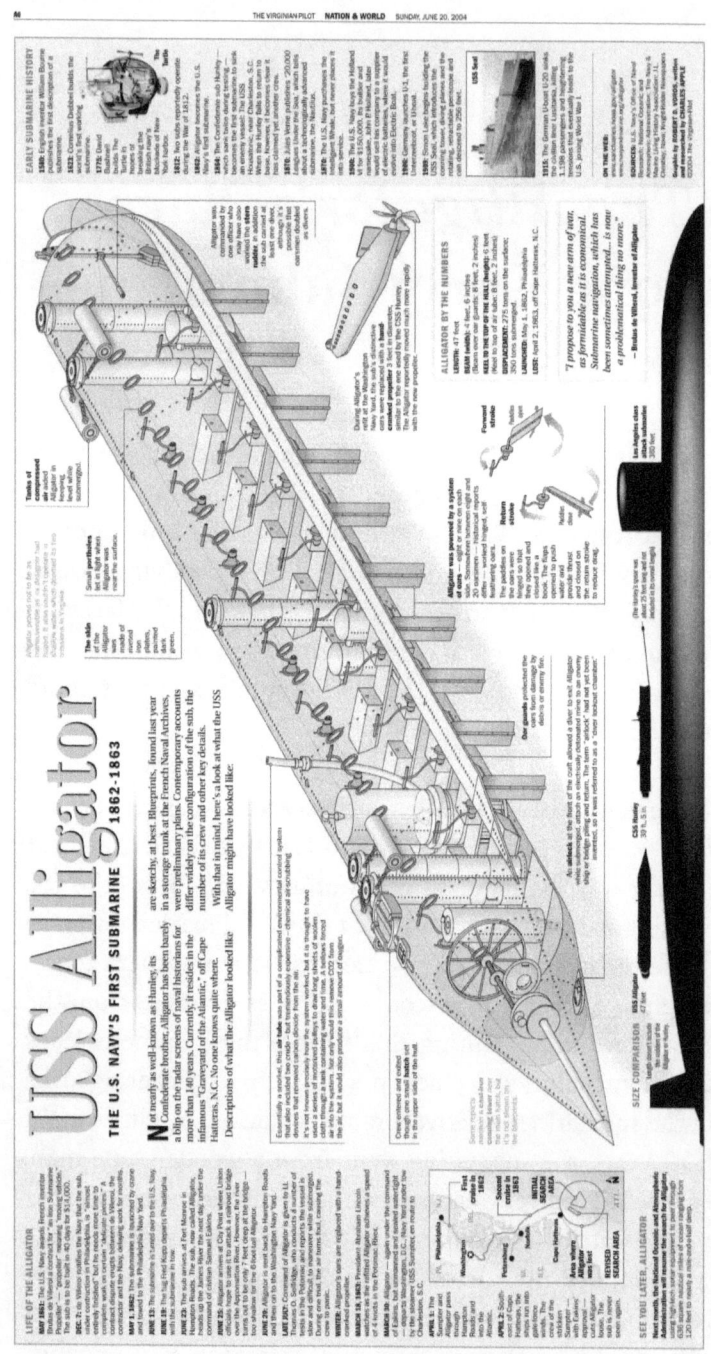

Schematic of the USS *Alligator* and its comparison to other submarines as published in the *Virginia Pilot* in June 2004.

A Long Fascination

The interest in submarine capabilities reaches back much farther than the American Revolution. Research reveals that people living in the Middle Ages considered, or at least conceived on paper, a type of craft that was able to operate beneath the water's surface. But there is no evidence that any attempts were made at construction. Not until the later part of the Renaissance, circa 1600, was a submarine-type craft possibly built. Prior to that, divers used simple diving bells to salvage sunken ships in shallow water. These diving bells certainly spurred the imagination and early thinking that eventually led to the submarine. In the 1700s, submarine experimentation began in some European maritime nations. For example, England had, by 1727, patented a dozen or more types of submarine designs; and records show that two "submarines" were built in France by 1700. Even the Cossacks got into the act, constructing a type of diving bell for reconnaissance and infiltration via rivers. Fertile minds were at work in many places.

At the outset of the 1800s, the dreamers and engineers waited in the wings for the century to change and the Industrial Revolution to begin. The *Alligator* was part of the early submarine lineage that emerged in 1800 with Robert Fulton's *Nautilus*, built for the French government to sink warships. Neither the French nor the British thought much of the *Nautilus*, and, by 1804, it disappeared from the record. Over the next several decades, the Industrial Revolution gathered momentum, and submarine development moved along with it. Submerged crafts were being developed in various places around the world, primarily in Europe, but also in other places, such as Latin America. In 1836, the young French engineer Brutus de Villeroi — the future designer of the *Alligator* more than two decades later — experimented with designs for a submarine.

By mid-century, the pace of submarine development quickened, and it was among this period's group of designs and vessels that the *Alligator* emerged. The similarity of the submarines from this time suggests that an informal community of submarine advocates, designers, and builders were exchanging ideas, but little information exists to support this notion. If such a community existed, Brutus de Villeroi must have been part of it. However, little was really known about de Villeroi's life until 2018, when Chuck Veit published his excellent book, *Natural Genius: Brutus de Villeroi and the U.S. Navy's First Submarine*[3], after more than a decade of research. Brutus de Villeroi, just like his creation, the *Alligator*, was finally rediscovered. The book is a good read and illustrates the vibrant scientific community and inventors of this period.

A Unique Submarine

What set the *Alligator* apart from the other submarines and designs during the American Civil War-era were its technological innovations. These included a lockout chamber that allowed divers to walk on the bottom to plant mines on structures and warships; an air-recirculation system to scrub carbon dioxide from the air in the submarine; buoyancy devices to maintain depth and stability; and even glass prisms in the "port holes" to let light into the submarine when it was on the surface. Many of these innovations became known only when the search to rediscover the *Alligator* uncovered long-buried documents and facts. One document that proved to be vital was Brutus de Villeroi's letter, dated May 1, 1863, petitioning the French Admiralty to commission him to build a submarine for the French Navy. In this letter, he extolled the technological features of the submarine he had built for the U.S.

---

3 Lulu Press, Inc., Morrisville, North Carolina; 2018.

Navy — the *Alligator* — and included its blueprints and cross sections. In his own words, de Villeroi described the innovations he built into the *Alligator*:

> The main improvements that I contributed to make this system desirable are:
>
> I. The air purification system and at-will renewal systems for the crewmen's breathing.
> II. The ability to immerse and emerge at will without losing ballast, and by navigating at the surface like an ordinary ship.
> III. The ability to regularly maintain while in movement a set depth underwater to lead a torpedo under a ship or to pierce an enemy ship.
> IV. While the ship is submerged, men can get in and out of the ship without having to bring the ship to the surface.
> V. While submerged maintain men outside the ship to operate secret missions for 15-20 minutes.
> VI. To reach a speed of 6-8 kilometers/hour.
> VII. Have motion independent from any accidents to lateral wheels and propellers.
> VIII. To go backwards as needed and to easily change tack at a small radius.
> IX. To collide a ship underwater in order to pierce it or to blow it up with the use of the device number 8 in the blueprint, and to damage the ship enough to sink it.
> X. Finally, when facing an unforeseen danger while underwater, to be able to instantaneously release 1500K of ballast attached at three different points inside the ship.
>
> With the advantages presented by this system, it is easy to foresee the results obtained with a well-built and well-manned submarine ship, against any kind of vessel. It is therefore a means to successfully conduct a maritime war almost without men or equipment.

No other submarines being built at this time are known to have this array of technological innovations. Yet, only recently has the *Alligator*, the U.S. Navy's first investment in a submarine, begun to claim its rightful place in submarine

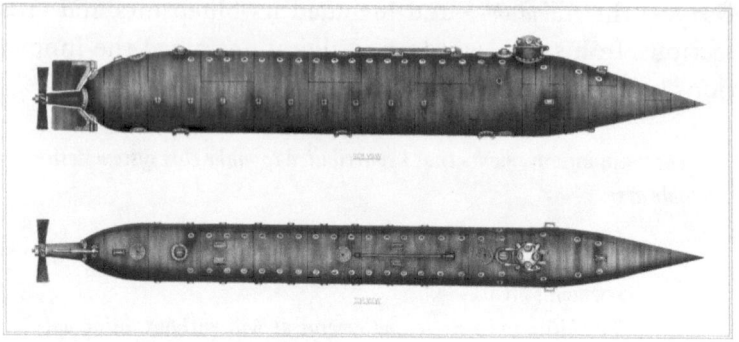

Illustration of how the *Alligator* may have looked by Christley, Smalley, Merriman, and Hines.

evolution and U.S. naval history. A number of books document the development of submarines of this period. Two particularly relevant and excellent books are: *Submarine Warfare in the Civil War* by Mark K. Ragan[4] and *Misadventures of a Civil War Submarine: Iron, Guns, and Pearls* by James P. Delgado[5]. A great amount of information on submarine development is also available online. Hence, it is not necessary to reprise the full story of 19th century submarines here.

Nonetheless, describing the starts, stops, and drama surrounding the USS *Alligator*'s journey to life, especially as documented in Chuck Viet's book, illustrates the difficulties the designers, engineers, and advocates of these new "infernal machines" faced up until the dawn of the 20th century. The Industrial Revolution pushed the edges of technology in such a dramatic fashion that it forever changed civilization and culture. The contributions of this period's submarine builders hold a particular place in the era's aspirations and imaginations. Indeed, Brutus de Villeroi and others like him were pioneers, much like those pursuing space travel today.

---

4 Da Capo Press, New York, New York; 2009.
5 Texas A&M University Press, College Station, Texas; 2012.

CHAPTER 3

Serendipity in the South Pacific

Rear Admiral Jay Cohen, his wife Nancy, and I first met in Brisbane, Australia, in May 2002 in a cluttered area near the gate for an airplane we were about to board to Guadalcanal and the Solomon Islands. We were there because Bob Ballard was about to undertake a National Geographic Society-sponsored expedition to search for John F. Kennedy's PT-109, lost in the upper Solomon Islands during WWII. I was there primarily because Bob and his team had been doing expeditions in National Marine Sanctuaries, for which I was director, and he knew my interests. This would be my third expedition to the Solomon Islands, and I was happy to be invited. Besides, I thought I could be of some help. I knew most of Bob's team and had operated with them before. I also thought my knowledge of the Solomon Islands, particularly my first-hand experience in the area where the expedition was going, might be useful.

At that time, RADM Cohen — or Jay, as I call him — was the head of the Office of Naval Research (ONR) of the U.S. Navy, and he knew Bob well. Jay would go on to become the longest-serving commanding officer in ONR's history and to profoundly influence research, both inside and outside of the Navy, for decades. The Navy had sponsored development of Bob's technology for a long time, and the PT-109 was a U.S. Navy vessel. Bob wisely always had an eye for his sponsors, and, when he could, he invited them along. By happenstance, Jay and Nancy were vacationing in Australia and Bob asked them to join the expedition. When we met that day in Brisbane, I was surprised to learn that Jay and Nancy were on the expedition. I don't recall seeing many Americans during my previous expeditions in the Solomons. Maybe they had been around, and I just hadn't run into them. This particular expedition, however, was anything but ordinary. It was also the platform for a documentary film production. There were more than a dozen others at the gate who were going, and more would be meeting us at Honiara on Guadalcanal. I won't say it was a traveling circus, but it certainly had the feel of a traveling entourage. Most likely, no one in the group had ever been to the Solomon Islands, except for Bob, and no one will likely ever return. For many, it was an opportunity-of-a-lifetime experience. But all that is another story. In the end, the National Geographic film was made, and a book was written about the expedition. Besides, what happens in the Solomon Islands stays in the Solomon Islands.

The pivotal moment that initiated the search for the USS *Alligator* happened one day on board the Australian vessel that National Geographic had leased for the expedition, *Gray Scout*. It was a small vessel and there was barely room for the gear and equipment crammed aboard and a few berths. Most everyone slept ashore at the Gizo Hotel, which was the only place to stay on the remote Island of Gizo. I had stayed there three years before. On this particular day, the ship was "mowing the lawn," which means it was slowly towing a side-scan sonar unit along prescribed survey lines – a pattern similar to mowing a lawn. In this maneuver, the ship basically goes back and forth, following the survey lines. When the sonar detects an anomaly on the bottom, researchers record the position, capture a sonar image, place it in a file, and the ship moves on.

The *Gray Scout* operating in the upper Solomon Islands in 2002.

After the entire area is sonar-mapped, the team analyzes the anomalies, or targets, and reviews plans for the next phase, when the vessel tows remotely operated vehicles with cameras to identify the targets of interest. This is how Bob eventually found the PT-109, along with some pretty interesting Japanese destroyers that sunk during the same period.

Mowing the lawn can get boring, as it was on this day when the *Alligator* came into our lives. Without much to do, Jay, Bob, and I sat at a table in the small galley off of the control room. Three or four people, including Dwight Coleman who was Bob's protégé, stood watch in the control room and fixated on their monitors. Three years later Dwight would sail with us on a U.S. Navy ship in the hunt for the *Alligator*. Occasionally, someone in the control room radioed the bridge for a course correction. In those days, only a few ships had dynamic positioning with satellites. The *Gray Scout* did not, and it took a lot of skill and experience to keep her on station. The

Bob Ballard, *standing*, in the *Gray Scout* control room during operations, while Dwight Coleman, *back and center*, sits at a monitor.

watch-keepers in the control room and the captain on the bridge essentially coordinated a three-dimensional ballet. I periodically stood watch at the monitor keeping track of the sonar unit's depth off the bottom and remotely adjusted the winch on the stern as necessary. Fortunately, we didn't run into anything on my watch. Other watch-standers weren't so lucky.

First Mention

I think Jay, Bob, and I had exhausted our conversation, and that is saying something because we all like to talk. We had spent a lot of time together during the last week or so and were starting to retell our stories. Then Jay brightened up, leaned over the table, and said, "I'm sure you guys can help me because you're both in the business, right?" I thought Jay was giving us both too much credit for something, especially me. He proceeded to describe Nancy's recent discovery of an article in a Civil War history magazine about a Navy submarine, a secret weapon during the American Civil War, called the *Alligator*. Jay continued, "I've been a submariner for most of my Navy career and I have never heard of it. We all know the *Holland* was the first U.S. Navy submarine in 1902, right?" Bob and I looked at one another with that blank expression of being caught off guard and said, almost in unison, "Never heard of it." Jay gave us the few details he remembered, and then something distracted us.

Later, after dinner at the Gizo Hotel, Nancy, Jay, and I talked further about the article. It didn't offer much information or detail, but it featured a crude sketch of this *Alligator* submarine, taken from an 1862 Philadelphia newspaper story. Here we were, on an expedition to find a needle in a haystack in the South Pacific, discussing an entirely different and even smaller vessel that wasn't even in the historic record. We weren't sure, at that point, that the *Alligator* actually existed. Jay and I decided we would do a little digging when we got back to the States. We made plans to have lunch soon after our return and to figure out how to follow up on the article. Bob was so wrapped up in the search for the PT-109 that we didn't talk further with him about the *Alligator*. We agreed, however, we would let him know what we found out, if anything.

The expedition to find the PT-109 was a great experience for everyone. I got to dive on the shipwrecks in the area I wanted to revisit and to do a little exploring of an unknown Japanese underwater craft — a lot had been going on among

They started it all. RADM Cohen, *left*, and the author at the First Symposium on the USS *Alligator*, 18 months after their initial conversation about a mysterious Civil War Navy submarine.

these islands during WWII — as well as to help out a little, as I had hoped. Of course, Bob found the remains of the PT-109 just as time was running out!

Unbeknownst to us, the Solomon Islands government had collapsed during the expedition. We were nearly stranded in the upper Solomon Islands. No one knew problems were afoot until a few days before we were to head back to Guadalcanal. I should have recognized the signs around Honiara, but I just wasn't paying enough attention. Since my last visit, certain things, such as villages and huts, had vanished from surrounding areas. Only one overused Twin Otter aircraft was in service. Patrol boats, once crisp and clean, no longer carried guns and were tied-up as derelicts. In the moment, I had probably just chalked it up to "it's the South Pacific." Some anxious moments and confusion, especially for some of our colleagues, ensued. But everyone eventually got back to Guadalcanal and made it to Brisbane. Jay, Nancy and I were on the last Twin Otter flight out of Gizo, at least for a while.

Jay, Nancy, and I bonded during the expedition. Sometimes being thrown together far from home does that. Whatever it is, we remain good friends today. Back in Washington, D.C., Jay and I would go on to have that lunch and put our heads together, and the rest is its own history — the search for the USS *Alligator*.

CHAPTER 4

Like Minds Go to Work

Life was immediately hectic back in Washington. No matter how well RADM Cohen and I had prepared our respective organizations to carry on during our absences in the South Pacific, running nationwide organizations is a 24/7 job, and things pile up. I know I felt this, but it must have been doubly hectic for RADM Cohen. He was responsible for the U.S. Navy's research worldwide and managed more than a billion dollars of taxpayer money. But he never complained, and somehow, he always found time when it came to finding a place in history for the U.S. Navy's first submarine, the USS *Alligator*.

RADM Cohen's fascination with submarines began long before mine, starting when he was a midshipman at the U.S. Naval Academy and one of the early Trident Scholars. Initially, the Trident Scholars program was designed to determine if particularly talented midshipmen could independently conduct high-quality and meaningful research. Jay's research was on deep-submergence submarines, a new and exciting field that was vital to the Navy. I'm sure he helped prove the value of the Trident Scholars program, then in its experimental phase, when his research was featured in the *Proceedings of the United States Naval Institute*[6]. So, it's no wonder that he went into the submarine service, commanded nuclear submarines, rose to command the ONR, and then became fascinated by

---
6 See the January 1, 1969, issue of the Proceedings.

this unknown technological underwater marvel — the USS *Alligator*. Eventually, we enlisted a group of contemporary Trident Scholars at the U.S. Naval Academy to join in the hunt.

At the time, I had dived on a number of submarine wrecks, studied a little about submarine exploits, and even ridden on a few submarines. But compared to Jay I was not only a Johnny-come-lately to the world of submarines but an amateur as well. Jay's enthusiasm, however, certainly motivated me to look into the *Alligator* story. Besides, I had the authority to investigate historic shipwrecks of interest to the United States due to my position at NOAA. It also helped that I was developing a Maritime Heritage Program comprised of maritime archeologists and historians. Jay and I joined forces, and I would follow him on the trail as far as it took us and everyone else we pulled in.

It didn't take long to get the ball rolling. I don't know who got started first, but it was probably RADM Cohen since he could simply order someone to search for information and clues about the USS *Alligator*. He had a couple of reserve officers on staff he thought might be of use. In my case, it was a little different in that I had to convince a few members of my staff to get unofficially involved, given their other assignments. In the end, this wasn't difficult; the *Alligator* mystery was compelling to the historians, marine archeologists, and staff of the emerging Maritime Heritage Program.

First Steps

Within a few weeks of our return from the South Pacific, RADM Cohen assigned Captain Woody Berzins of his public affairs staff to oversee two ONR interns from the University of Virginia to look for background information on the USS *Alligator*. I similarly prompted a few individuals on my staff, particularly historian Bruce Terrell, to do the same. Bruce was our organization's leading historian. He also had a great personal interest in the Civil War and had worked on a number of Civil War-related projects. Bruce is from Richmond, Virginia, and his interest in the Civil War probably began when he first took a breath. Yet, given all his Civil War-related endeavors, he had never come across even a mention of the USS *Alligator*. But he certainly knew where to look and who to talk to. The problem, however, remained that, at first blush, no one we spoke to had heard of the *Alligator*.

This quickly changed when Commander (CMDR) Richard Poole, also on RADM Cohen's staff, tracked down Jim Christley, a retired Navy senior chief and U.S. Navy veteran submariner. After more than a decade of personal research, Jim wrote the *Alligator* article published in *Civil War Times Illustrated* magazine, which Nancy Cohen read, triggering all the events that followed.

As Jim tells it, it was sometime in 1979 that he came across an obscure reference to an unknown Frenchmen named Brutus de Villeroi and his "Submarine Propeller," aka the *Alligator*. Jim was instantly fascinated. Maybe the term *submarine* originally attracted him — after all he was a veteran submariner. Whatever it was, he subsequently dedicated himself to learning as much as he could about this mysterious submarine. He discovered a 1938 article about the *Alligator* by Luis Bollander in the *Proceedings of the Naval Institute*, which reinforced his interest. When CMDR Poole contacted Jim and explained our interest in knowing more about the USS *Alligator* featured in his article and possibly trying to find it, Jim was all in. He became a key member of what would become known as the USS *Alligator* Team or simply Team *Alligator*. As such, he joined a cadre of naval officers, archeologists, historians, scientists, and new enthusiasts with whom he could pursue his passion. Jim was no longer alone on his quest.

CMDR Poole also contacted Mark Ragan, the author of *Submarine Warfare in the Civil War*, who knew a little about the *Alligator*. But it was Mark's comprehensive knowledge of all things submarine during the Civil War that confirmed the value to U.S. Naval history of re-discovering the USS *Alligator*. This propelled us even further, and Mark became part of the evolving Team *Alligator*. We soon discovered a small circle of enthusiasts who knew something about the submarine, including descendants of Samuel Eakins, who played an important role in its short life. One enthusiast, Mrs. Alice Smith of Delanco, New Jersey, spent a great deal of time trying to identify the crew members assigned to the *Alligator*. Even so, Jim Christley's piece remained our primary source of information. There simply weren't any details about the *Alligator* itself beyond a fanciful sketch of an "Infernal Machine" on the water that appeared in a Philadelphia newspaper in 1861. The Infernal Machine sketch wasn't even of the USS *Alligator*, but rather an earlier Brutus de Villeroi submarine — the Submarine Propeller — that he was experimenting with on the Delaware River. We'd made progress for sure, but we needed to know so much more about everything. In truth, we had no real plan on how to proceed, but RADM Cohen and I kept sending out tentacles to see who and what we could turn up.

By early summer, CMDR Poole organized a full-court press at the Library of Congress, the National Archives, and the Naval Historical Center, now known as the Naval History and Heritage Command, to search for documents related to the USS *Alligator* and/or Brutus de Villeroi. Various individuals lent a hand, including Jim Christley, Mark Ragan, Bruce Terrell, and others who knew the ropes of doing research at these institutions. The effort immediately yielded results and unveiled secrets about the USS *Alligator*. For example, over 200 potentially relevant letters and documents — all handwritten — were identified at the National Archives. Reproductions of these documents are now at the U.S. Navy's Submarine Force Library and Museum in Groton, Connecticut[7]. Most of the bits and pieces to begin to tell the story of the USS *Alligator* were now in hand, and it took time and a lot of eyes to fit them together. But one letter was pivotal to pushing forward the idea that we might actually be able to find the USS *Alligator*.

The letter, dated April 1863, was sent to the Secretary of the Navy. It describes in detail the fateful event that occurred when the vessel towing the USS *Alligator* south to Charleston and Savannah cut the submarine loose during a storm off the Diamond Shoals of Cape Hatteras. The letter was written by Acting Master J.D. Winchester of the USS *Sumpter*, which had towed the submarine. It contains a fascinating description of the peril and drama aboard the USS *Sumpter* during the storm. Winchester also makes it clear that the decision to cut the USS *Alligator* loose and save the ship was made jointly between himself and Samuel Eakins, who was responsible for getting the USS *Alligator* south for her new mission. There is no record that a board of inquiry investigated the loss of the *Alligator*, and this letter stands as the only explanation. Most importantly, the *Sumpter's* logbook identifies the last position taken by the ship before the storm. For the first time we knew approximately where the *Alligator* was likely set adrift. This position information initiated our first speculation as to where the *Alligator* may have come to rest.

---

7 A few documents have been transcribed and appear in the Appendices.

Well-kept Secret

With the documents uncovered by Team *Alligator* and enthusiasts, we were able to write a history of the *Alligator's* short life — from the shipyard to the grave — and the individuals, besides Brutus de Villeroi, who played important roles. But a key piece of the puzzle was still missing. We hadn't found any blueprints, construction drawings, building instructions, or plans from the shipyard where the USS *Alligator* was built — or from the U.S. Navy itself. This begs the question: Why didn't the Navy have these documents, or copies of them, on file as they do for most vessels they have constructed?

One explanation might be that the U.S. Navy viewed the USS *Alligator* as such an important secret weapon that Navy sources collected all documentation about the submarine so it would not fall into Confederate hands. At the time, the Confederates were also struggling to build submarines. In fact, we discovered correspondence from the Navy to de Villeroi, requesting he take an oath or affirm in writing the details of his secret and to deposit said secret in a sealed envelope with the Chief of the Bureau of Yards and Docks[8]. Perhaps after the *Alligator* was lost the Navy's concern for secrecy ultimately led them to destroy the *Alligator* construction plans and related documents. On the other hand, those papers might exist in some dusty, forgotten, "secret" place, waiting to be discovered. Whatever the case, we found nothing until later when desperation led us across the Atlantic Ocean to Paris, but more on that later.

Initially, we knew very little about Brutus de Villeroi, aside from the 1860 Census records that put him in Philadelphia with a self-described profession of "Genius." We eventually learned more about him, beginning with an April 25, 1861, article in

---
8 See Appendix C.

Article 6 -- No Title
Saturday Evening Post (1839-1885); May 25, 1861; APS Online
pg. 3

VILLEROI'S SUBMARINE PROPELLER---EXTERIOR VIEW.

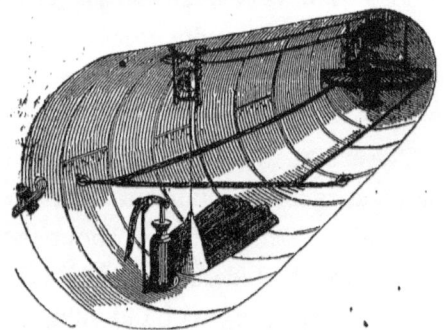

VILLEROI'S SUBMARINE PROPELLER---INTERIOR VIEW.

We give this week engravings of an aquatic monster which recently caused no small degree of excitement among the very unexcitable citizens of this remarkably sober Quaker City. Our neighbors of the *Inquirer* well say, that "never since the Battle of the Kegs has the river front of Philadelphia been the scene of such a peculiar excitement."

At an early hour in the morning rumors spread like wildfire among the inflammable population crowding our wharves, that a monster, half aquatic, half metal, and wholly incomprehensible, had been captured by the Harbor Police, and had been safely chained at the foot of Noble street pier.

Forthwith the pier became the grand centre of attraction. The crowd increased hourly, the spectators flocking to see the amphibious and ambiguous creature. All sorts of speculations were freely indulged in as to the uses and purposes of the lengthy iron circular continuance, all tending, however, to the belief that it was designed to aid and assist Jeff. Davis in the benevolent occupation of transferring Federal vessels of war into flying morsels of wood and iron, i. e., blowing them up, while every one concurred in the opinion that it was "very like a whale."

The monster itself, on a close inspection, proved to be a submarine propeller, invented by Monsieur De Villeroi, a French gentleman, who has devoted many years to experiments in this direction. The hull was built about two years ago, at the machine works of Neall, Matthews & More, on Bush Hill, and at that time was reputed to be under the joint ownership of its inventor and Mr. Girard, a connection of the benefactor, and one of the claimants to his vast estates. In its unfinished condition it attracted the attention of the Hon. Wm. H. Witte, who induced its removal to the Penn Iron Works of Reaney, Neafie & Co., where it was supplied with a propelling apparatus.

It is made of ¾-inch boiler iron, shaped like a segar, sharp at both ends, and about forty feet long by five in diameter, and is propelled by a screw, worked by hand, from the inside. On the top is a copper basin-shaped lid, which has glasses for the men to see out, and large enough for a man's head. It covers the entrance. Seven men are required to work the boat. The inside is partially filled with air pumps, force pumps, &c.

It is submerged by pumping water into the lower compartment, and it is claimed can be kept under for twenty-four hours, and propelled five miles an hour. It has been down for a period of one hour and thirteen minutes. It is intended for scuttling or blowing up vessels, and report says the inventor was offered one million of dollars for it by the Russian Government, to destroy the Allied fleet during the Crimean war, but, being a good Frenchman, he declined.

The machine has attracted the attention of a number of parties at different times, who imagined they discovered in the invention a speculation which would yield a handsome return for any outlay. Mr. Martin F. Thomas, an estimable citizen, invested capital in the project some time since, with a view of defraying a means to cleanse the Great Eastern during her first visit to this country. A proposition to this effect was submitted to the Directors, and the attempt would no doubt have resulted successfully, had they not preferred an English "gridironing" to an American scraping process.

Since that time, the submarine vessel has for divers reasons been stationed in sundry places. Of these were Marcus Hook, New Castle, and Delanco on the Rancocas. A number of experiments were tried, with a view of adopting it to recovering goods from wrecks, and examining the bottoms of rivers, but from all that we can gather, the machine has proved, so far, an utter failure for all practical purposes.

The first information that the police had of the appearance of the vessel opposite our city, was that it was, about midnight, taking in a quantity of pig lead, which was to be used as ballast, in some experiments which were contemplated. At the time of its seizure, it was under the charge of a young Frenchman, named Alexander Rhodes, and Henry Kriner, an American, who were arrested. They stated that the machine was to be taken to the Navy Yard to be examined by Government officers to ascertain whether it could be made serviceable in naval operations. Its movements and this intention have not been kept a secret, and at any other time than the present, no excitement would have been created by its appearance.

The views which we present are of the interior and exterior. They will convey to our readers a better idea of the novelty than any written description. Its seizure was very necessary—for it might be, in dangerous hands, a dangerous customer. If it is what it claims to be—and even if at present a failure, keen wits might perhaps convert it into a success. The blockading fleet will of course keep a watch for such ugly customers.

Illustration of Brutus de Villeroi's "Submarine Propeller" from the *Philadelphia Saturday Evening Post,* dated May 25, 1861.

Philadelphia's *Saturday Evening Post*, describing the "Infernal Machine" on the water as reported by citizens, and from letters and correspondence that Team *Alligator* uncovered. But all of this pertained to only a small slice of de Villeroi's life around the Civil War years. By all accounts, he was an irascible individual who thought highly of himself. So, despite our best efforts, Brutus de Villeroi, like his creation, still remained elusive at this time.

Could it be Found?

As is usually the case when embarking on a journey of discovery, we were optimistic. Since we now had some position information, we thought we might be able to go out and find the USS *Alligator* directly. After all, isn't that what our community knows how to do? And hadn't we found another needle

Jim Christley's painting of the USS *Alligator* starting its tow south behind the USS *Sumpter*.

Jim Christley's painting of the USS *Alligator* towed by the USS *Sumpter* before the storm.

in a haystack, the PT-109, several months before? Maybe we already had enough research in hand to find the *Alligator*.

By the end of that first summer, we plotted an *Alligator* search area on a nautical chart, based primarily on the information in J.D. Winchester's letter. Captain Berzins (USN), CMDR Poole (USN), Bruce Terrell, and NOAA Corps officers Capt. Craig McLean and Lieutenant J.G. Jeremy Weirich reviewed the letter. They focused on the description of storm conditions at the time the USS *Alligator* was cut loose. But it was Craig and Jeremy, both experienced mariners with recent time at sea, along with help from Bruce Terrel, who took the first stab at defining a search area. No one had ever looked for the *Alligator*, and, given all the uncertainty, this first guess was as good as any. At least we had a search area, and this — a circle on a chart — was another of the steps moving forward interest in the USS *Alligator*.

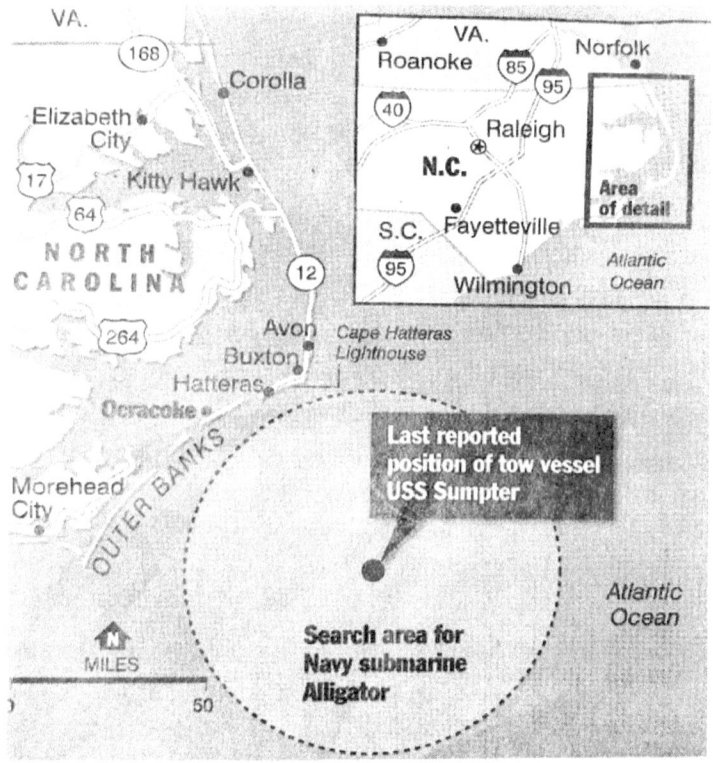

Map showing both the USS *Sumpter*'s last reported position and the initial search area for the USS *Alligator*.

Craig, Jeremy, and I were colleagues and friends. In fact, Craig and I worked closely together when I first came to what is now NOAA's Office of National Marine Sanctuaries. He had been my deputy for over a year and was much wiser than me in Washington's political ways. I learned a lot from him, and together I think we made the NOAA leadership at the time nervous. Subsequently Craig was assigned a research ship to put into service and command. He was eventually promoted to captain. We remain close today, even as dive buddies exploring shipwrecks. By the time the *Alligator* came into our lives, Craig had returned to NOAA headquarters and was appointed the first director of NOAA's new Office of Ocean Exploration. Of course, he immediately recruited Jeremy[9]. It didn't take much convincing to get them both involved in the *Alligator* project, and it even fit into Craig's new mission.

Despite our early efforts to define a search area, the Winchester letter made it clear how difficult finding the *Alligator* was going to be. The *Sumpter*'s last reported position was taken hours before the storm. How far from that position the ship had steamed and was driven by the storm when it cut the *Alligator* loose is anybody's guess. We had scant information on the 1863 storm's winds and surface currents. In addition, we had no idea of the *Alligator*'s condition when she was released. It was the *Sumpter* that was in trouble, not necessarily the *Alligator*, when the ship and submarine parted ways.

We presume the *Alligator* took on water during the storm and perhaps wallowed, making the tow more difficult. On the other hand, the *Alligator* was a submarine sealed with the best gasket technology of the time. The questions then became: How much water could the *Alligator* take on, and what was her state of buoyancy when the tow line was severed? There were also other confounding variables. For example, the *Alligator* may have drifted for hours or even days, pushed by the wind and currents. Plus, when she eventually sank, she might have been in the grasp of the powerful Gulf Stream current that runs along the East Coast. To compound the problem further, our knowledge of the *Alligator* itself was speculative at this point. In any case, we needed more in-depth knowledge and analyses of the meteorological and oceanographic aspects of the storm's conditions, as well as technical details about the *Alligator* itself.

---

9 At the time of this writing, 2024, Jeremy is now the Director of NOAA's Office of Ocean Exploration.

Trident Scholars

We needed to better define our search area. Our first attempt was at the U.S. Naval Academy in Annapolis, Maryland. Like so many things surrounding the USS *Alligator* project, this came about through happenstance. I was teaching dark-water scuba diving at the Naval Academy to the midshipmen in the Oceanography Club. LCDR Michiko Martin was the club's advisor. During our training sessions, I got to know her fairly well and told her about our joint Navy/NOAA USS *Alligator* project. I also described the meteorological and oceanographic analysis issues and explained that we didn't have anyone to dig into them. Always a problem-solver, Michiko suggested that the senior midshipmen in the Naval Academy's Trident Scholarship program and the oceanography instructors at the academy could help take on the challenge. I didn't know that Naval Academy instructors and midshipmen had helped in a similar project — the search for the USS *Monitor* — decades earlier. The USS *Monitor* site became the first National Marine Sanctuary. So it seemed fitting to ask the Naval Academy to help out yet again.

I checked in with RADM Cohen, who was a Trident Scholar back when he was at the Naval Academy. He thought involving the Trident Scholars was an inspired idea and concluded it would also help to raise awareness of the USS *Alligator* project across the entire Navy. With RADM Cohen's support, the Trident Scholars took on the project with Michiko and her colleague at the Naval Academy, oceanography professor Peter Guth, as their advisors. It was November 2002, only five months since that first discussion over coffee in the *Sea Scout* galley in the South Pacific. Things were looking up. The Trident Scholars would begin working on the *Alligator*

First USS *Alligator* poster created for public distribution.

questions at the onset of their new term, beginning in January 2003 and going through April.

LCDR Martin was destined to play a larger role in the search for the USS *Alligator*, when she left the U.S. Navy to work at NOAA as the director of education in the Office of National Marine Sanctuaries. She researched the office and what we did, as well as learned a lot from our long conversations during the dark-water scuba training at the academy. When Michiko decided she needed a career change, she responded to our job announcement. Michiko is a Naval Academy graduate and has an outstanding record as a Naval officer. We were fortunate to get her.

Reorganizing The Team

With momentum growing from the tentacles RADM Cohen and I put into motion in early summer, we now needed to get better organized and devise a plan for continuing the *Alligator* investigation and search. Toward the end of November, CMDR Poole began organizing the first meeting of a steering committee to plan and coordinate our efforts. The meeting, held two months later in February 2003 at the ONR, brought together Navy and NOAA personnel involved in the investigation thus far. Jim Christley and Mark Ragan also attended. It was a good start, and our early discussions focused on creating a USS *Alligator* Symposium to share our discoveries. But our primary goal was to further stimulate the interests of others. Three important actions came out of this meeting.

First, we drafted a brochure, *Secrets of the USS Alligator*, for external distribution. This signaled to the world that there was an official project underway to re-discover the story of the U.S. Navy's long-lost, secret, Civil War submarine. CMDR Poole took the lead on the brochure under the direction of RADM Cohen. Second, we decided that CMDR Poole and Jim Christley would make a two-day trip to Philadelphia to search both the National Archives facility and the Pennsylvania Historical Society for information on Brutus de Villeroi. After all, he lived and worked in Philadelphia and, as it turned out, passed away there in 1874. Our intrepid investigators uncovered additional personal information about Monsieur de Villeroi and located and photographed the row house where he lived. He appeared to be known and active in Philadelphia's inventor circles. But they found little additional information relative to the USS *Alligator*, and so we still didn't have any drawings, plans, or personal descriptions of his greatest invention. Lastly, we recognized our need to expand Team *Alligator*, and, thus, we planned a second, larger steering committee meeting for April.

The April meeting, also held at the ONR offices, included participants from ONR, NOAA, the Navy Historical Center, the Naval Academy, and other Team *Alligator* members, such as Jim Christley and Mark Ragan. The meeting lasted more than half a day, during which time the midshipmen Trident Scholars first presented their oceanographic analysis regarding the loss of the USS *Alligator*. Later that month, they presented their analysis at the Naval Academy. The midshipmen had done their best and got high marks for their work. But I realized the analysis necessary was beyond their scope of experience and would be a challenge for even the experts. In addition, a critical piece of information was still missing – the technical characteristics of the USS *Alligator* itself.

By May, almost exactly a year since RADM Cohen, Bob Ballard, and I initially conversed about the *Alligator* in the

South Pacific, we were approaching a dead end. We had no more leads to follow and interest was starting to wane. We needed something — a new find, or new lead. So far, the search had been interesting, but it would all be in vain if we couldn't uncover a stronger trail to the mysterious Brutus de Villeroi and his invention.

Chapter 5

Paris Is a City of Light

With no further USS *Alligator* leads to follow, RADM Cohen and I mulled over what to do next. There was nothing we, or others, could think of aside from following Brutus de Villeroi's trail back to his native country, France. RADM Cohen contacted the naval attaché at the U.S. Embassy in Paris and asked if their staff could look into de Villeroi. Naval officers are not typically trained in the skills of the historian; they also faced the challenges of doing research in France. It was a reach to think they could come up with much. It wasn't as though Brutus de Villeroi was a household name. Nevertheless, Paris would become a City of Light for us, piercing the darkness surrounding de Villeroi and his mysterious submarine.

Fortunately, a year or so before, I recruited NOAA scientist Catherine Marzin to join the Office of National Marine Sanctuaries — Catherine spoke fluent French. Working on her doctorate and interested in just about everything, she had a knack for asking penetrating questions. I considered her a scientific jack-of-all-trades, similar to a baseball utility player who could fit in wherever needed. Her cubicle was close to those of Bruce Terrell, our senior historian and an original member of Team *Alligator*, and Mike Overfield, a marine archeologist/historian who was pushing to get involved in the *Alligator* project. I think Catherine was living vicariously through Bruce and Mike, listening to the projects and schemes they debated on most days.

Catherine heard a lot about the *Alligator* from Bruce, Mike, and Michiko Martin, the former Navy lieutenant commander who joined NOAA and our office. There was no question that the mystery submarine fascinated Catherine, as did Brutus de Villeroi. She made sure that I knew she would help out in any way she could. Until that May, she had been on the periphery, but all that was about to change dramatically, placing her dead-center in the search for the *Alligator*.

Destination Paris

Catherine periodically traveled to France to visit her mother. We usually discussed these visits as I had to approve her leave, but I was also interested in her travels and family history. Catherine came from an illustrious French naval family. Sometime in April, I once again approved her leave to visit her mother. As serendipity would have it, this coincided with RADM Cohen and my decision to follow the de Villeroi trail to France.

The naval attaché at the embassy in Paris made some preliminary inquiries but found nothing. Opportunity was knocking for Catherine, and she was about to be in the right place at the right time. Hearing about our inquires in France, Catherine offered to add a week to her leave in order to travel to Paris and beat the sidewalks — visiting museums, archives, and naval offices looking for clues about de Villeroi. It didn't hurt that Catherine knew a bit about French naval history. She was the perfect person to seek out de Villeroi's trail in these French institutions. So, in April 2003, off she went on a mission to Paris resulting in a find that ranks among the great discoveries in U.S. maritime history.

We agreed that Catherine would email or phone every day and pass on anything she might uncover. Mike Overfield quickly volunteered to be her lead point of contact. Like all things he was involved in, Mike jumped in with both feet. He briefed me daily on his conversations with Catherine and passed on her frustrations, but always added, "Maybe tomorrow." Every day she reported that no one she spoke with had heard of Brutus de Villeroi, nor could they find anything about him in their files. Mike was a good anchor for her. He was, by nature, an out-of-the-box thinker and passed along ideas for Catherine to consider. He was always positive.

Catherine's search began to have the ring of another dead-end. But Mike remained optimistic and continued to encourage her. The last place Catherine visited before leaving Paris was the Service Historique de la Marine in Vincennes, outside of Paris. The people there hadn't heard of Brutus de Villeroi but said they would look further in their archives. Catherine was scheduled to return home the next day, without hearing even a whisper of de Villeroi. I am sure she believed that her efforts had been in vain. Then, on the morning of her last day, the Service Historique de la Marine called her. They found a box with de Villeroi's name scribbled on the side, and "Would she like to come in and see it?" She immediately returned to Vincennes to examine the box.

Discovery of a Lifetime

The Service Historique de la Marine is a French naval archive, housing all the French Navy's historic correspondence and documents related to ship building and construction. When Catherine arrived there, naval historian Alexandre Duplaix took her to a room where, sitting on a table, was a white box with de Villeroi's name handwritten on the side. The box had been stored in the archives, unopened, for more than a century. Prior to Catherine's inquiries, no one at Service Historique de la Marine even knew it was there. Like the USS *Alligator*, this box had been lost — at least until now.

Donning white gloves, Catherine examined the contents of the box. Apparently, every piece of correspondence between de Villeroi and someone in the French Admiralty had been placed and stored in this box. Of course, everything was written in French, and Catherine was exactly the right person to sift through the stack of fascinating personal and official documents. She concluded, judging by the nature of the correspondence, that Brutus de Villeroi was as irascible with the French Navy as he was with the U.S. Navy. After all, he was a self-declared genius. The documents revealed that de Villeroi consistently pushed hard to convince the French navy to build a submarine, and they always rejected him. Perhaps these failures were among the reasons we found him experimenting in Philadelphia in 1860.

In one letter, de Villeroi again petitioned the Admiralty to engage him to build a submarine because he believed the French Navy and Empire needed one to keep up with other nations. At this time, the sparks that ignited the Franco-Prussian War were in the air. To convince the Admiralty that he was the most qualified person to design and construct such a craft, he claimed to have successfully built a submarine for the Navy of the United States — something called the *Alligator*. The USS *Alligator*, however, was a top-secret weapon. Not only was the *Alligator* unknown to the French, but who could possibly even validate his claim? Certainly not the U.S. Navy.

Brutus de Villeroi must have anticipated something like this, because he kept a set of plans — in violation of his agreement with the U.S. Navy — when he walked off the unfinished job in Philadelphia in 1862[10]. In his final written exhortation to the Admiralty, explaining why he was so qualified, he included the plans he had kept for the submarine he built for the U.S. Navy. Catherine had found the "Holy Grail" — the original plans for the USS *Alligator*! What a moment that must have been for her!

When Catherine checked in and reported her discovery, it was hard to believe she had found the plans. How could this be? At best, we expected a few promising leads. Mike Overfield was over the moon and couldn't help but broadcast the news to anyone within earshot. He acted as if he had been at Catherine's side in Vincennes. I also felt the exhilaration, but I calmed Mike down a bit. We needed proof. I asked him to check back with Catherine to be absolutely certain. I wondered if Catherine really knew what ship's plans looked like. This find was so hard to believe after coming up empty-handed for almost a year. We had to be sure. Shortly, with the help of Alexandre Duplaix at the Service Historique de la Marine, we received photocopies. The plans were the real thing. This marked the pivotal point that changed forever the USS *Alligator* story, propelling the search to a new level in ways neither RADM Cohen nor I ever envisioned.

Everyone on Team *Alligator* wished they had been with Catherine in France. The feelings she experienced must have soared off the charts. I know she couldn't fully describe them, but from that moment forward, any mention of the word "*Alligator*" brought a smile to her face and put a twinkle in her eyes.

---

10 See Appendices A and B.

CHAPTER 6

New Momentum

Finding the original plans for the USS *Alligator* was totally unexpected, and it took time for the discovery to sink in and to digest it. Once word filtered out about Catherine's find in Paris, there was far more interest, from many quarters, about our little part-time project. But at the heart of people's attraction was the central question: "When do you expect to find the USS *Alligator* itself?" Clearly, the enthusiasm raised the stakes as to our next steps.

Well, we got ourselves into this, and now RADM Cohen and I needed to find creative ways to execute that next step — that is, to find the USS *Alligator*. One benefit of the increased attention was that it became easier to enlist others, particularly in the Navy and NOAA, to accept the challenge of finding the *Alligator*. It was, after all, the U.S. Navy's still missing and previously unknown first submarine, a state secret since the Civil War. It was seductive to want to be involved. Still, we hadn't conceived of any plans for an expedition to find the *Alligator*.

The heightened interest, however, opened new doors. In June 2003, we took an opportunity to briefly utilize the NOAA Ship *Thomas Jefferson*, a sophisticated hydrographic survey ship, to search for the *Alligator*. The *Thomas Jefferson* featured state-of-the-art multi-beam sonar. At least, we now thought we knew what to look for on the sea floor. The Navy

Blueprints' Discovery Sparks Search for Historic Sub

By MICHAEL E. RUANE
Washington Post Staff Writer

Catherine G. Marzin, a researcher with the federal government's National Marine Sanctuary Program, didn't know what awaited her that morning in the French naval archives outside Paris.

She was on the trail of one Brutus De Villeroi, a 19th-century French inventor who in 1861 designed the U.S. Navy's first submarine. The archives didn't have a biographical file on him. But the agency did have a box of his papers.

When Marzin, 34, opened the box in May and extracted file 3084, she was stunned. Inside were hand-drawn antique sketches of a vessel shaped like a fountain pen. It had a series of tiny portholes, a diver's chamber and strange, folding oars sticking out of its sides. "PLANS du Ba-

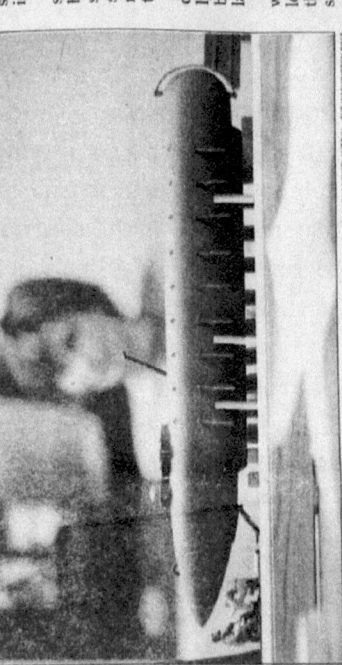

A model USS Alligator, the first Navy sub deployed to combat, is displayed in Silver Spring.

BY MICHEL LUTZKY — THE WASHINGTON POST

sank in a storm off Cape Hatteras, N.C., in 1863.

"It's like finding a photograph of a person you're doing historical research on, but you have no idea what they look like," said Jim Christley, a veteran of the Navy's submarine service and a submarine historian who has been researching the Alligator for years.

"It adds a lot of information that you didn't have before, stuff that you were only guessing about," Christley, 58, of Lisbon, Conn., said in a telephone interview last week.

"It answers questions for people who want to know hard facts: What does it look like? You can say: Here's what we think it looks like. This is what the designer intended."

Marzin's "finding those blueprints was an absolute jewel in the crown," he said. "And the fact that she had in being able

Article in the *Washington Post*, dated December 15, 2003.

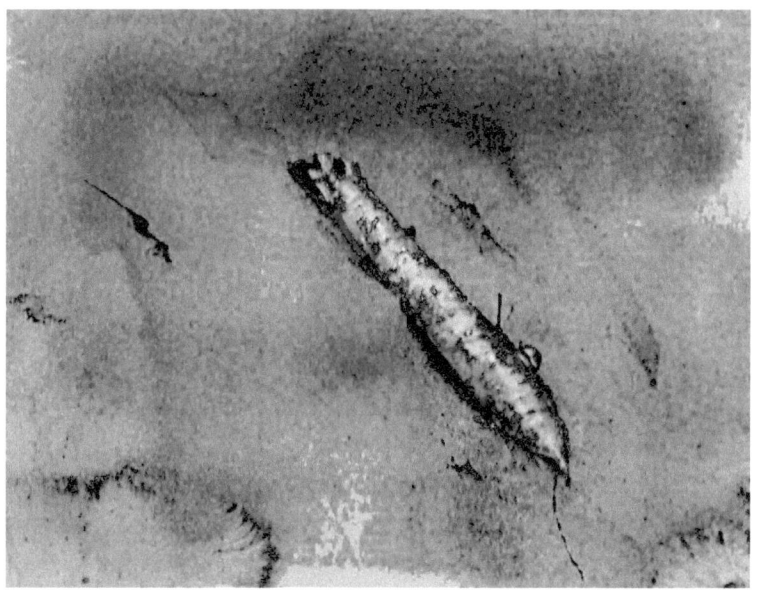

Jim Christley's painting shows how the *Alligator* may have looked at rest on the sea bottom.

The hydrographic vessel NOAA Ship *Thomas Jefferson*.

paid the operating costs and NOAA sponsored the rest. Thus, the *Thomas Jefferson* was deployed to survey the area initially defined by Captain Craig Mclean and Lieutenant J.G. Jeremy Weirich, both of the NOAA Corps. Maybe we would get lucky; sometimes discovery works that way. But, after cruising the area for 50 hours, the *Thomas Jefferson* hadn't discovered anything resembling the shape and dimensions of the *Alligator*. Clearly, finding the long-lost submarine was going to be a major challenge. There would be no short cut.

RADM Cohen and I both had experience on expeditions or missions to find vessels and objects in the ocean, and it was less than a year since the National Geographic expedition to find the PT-109 — another needle in a haystack. But that expedition involved a far smaller and better-defined search area than that surveyed by the *Thomas Jefferson*. We both knew how extremely difficult it is to find anything in the ocean, and something as small and buoyant as the *Alligator*, lost in a storm in 1863, might be impossible to locate. We lamented this problem many times. But it was in for a penny, in for a pound, and the search for the USS *Alligator* entered a new phase. If we were eventually going to sea to find the *Alligator*, we had to improve our "guesses" about where she might have settled on the bottom.

Clever Approach

Even if we knew exactly where she was, finding the *Alligator* would be difficult. Fortunately, NOAA is a leader in the mathematical modeling of how things placed in the ocean are transported by currents and winds, and where they wind up. I had worked for years with our premier modeling group in Seattle, operating in what is now the Office of Response and Restoration. I had also worked with Glen Watabayashi, who headed up the group. He was excited to be involved in the *Alligator* project, as was modeler Mark Hodges. They were the best modelers to take on the *Alligator* challenge. But we had one big problem: the models required accurate surface currents and wind data to make a reasoned prediction. There were little-to-no surface currents or wind observations taken during the storm of 1863. The sciences of modern oceanography and meteorology were still in their infancy at that time. How, then, could we possibly re-create this storm event and trace the possible path the *Alligator* may have taken during the storm?

This is where Michiko Martin's meteorological and oceanographic expertise and puzzle-solving interests came together. After finding only fragmental information about the currents and winds during the 1863 storm, Michiko discovered that a few lighthouses along the East Coast had collected air-pressure measurements as the historic nor'easter passed over them. Working with National Weather Service meteorologists, Michiko theorized that if a modern nor'easter could be identified that had

Left to right: The author, Catherine Marzin, and Michiko Martin study the USS *Alligator* plans.

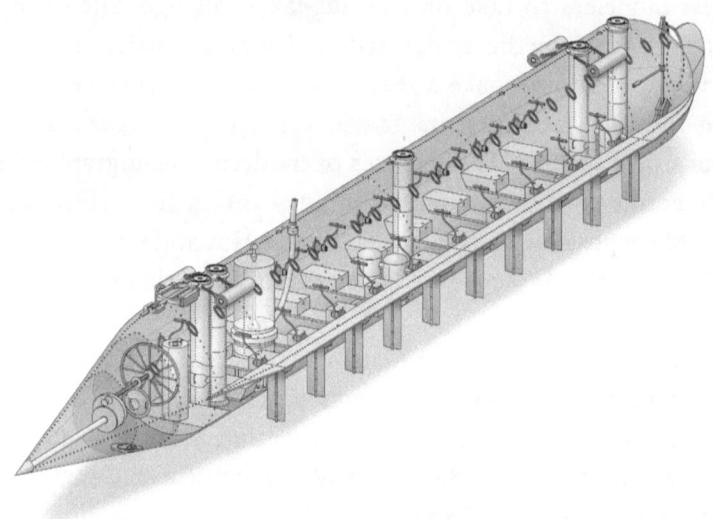

An artist's rendition of de Villeroi's plans illustrating the *Alligator*'s oar and rowing stations.

Rendition of an oar station as it appears in de Villeroi's plans.

Model by Jim Christley recreates the oar mechanism de Villeroi designed for the *Alligator*.

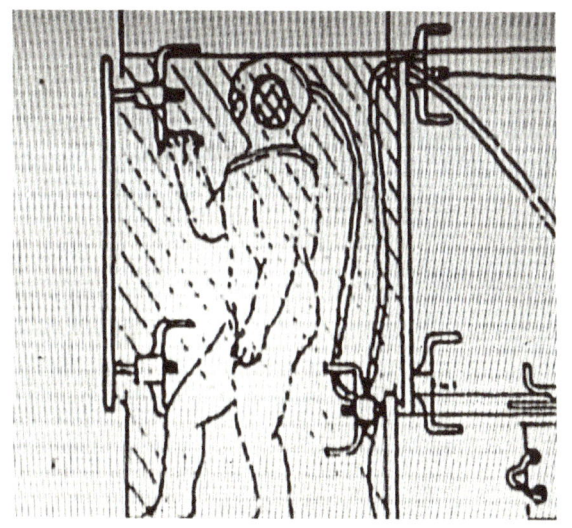

The *Alligator*'s lock-out chamber as shown on de Villeroi's plans.

air-pressure readings approximately matching those at the lighthouses, then the modern storm could be used as a reasonable approximation of the 1863 storm. Information from the USS *Sumpter*'s logs, such as its last known position and a water-temperature reading of 86 degrees Fahrenheit, along with details from Acting Master J.D. Winchester's April 1863 letter, provided the additional historic information needed to allow modelers to create alternative scenarios to predict where the *Alligator* may have traveled when the *Sumpter* cut her loose. I have made this approach sound easy, but it involved considerable work and was incredibly creative.

A Big Unknown

The *Alligator* was not a typical ship that was cut loose to sink. As a submarine, the *Alligator* was theoretically sealed and not necessarily in a sinking condition. Although she may have been leaking and filling during the tow and wallowing during the storm, making the tow even more threatening to the *Sumpter*'s survival. Still, how long had the *Alligator* remained on or just below the water's surface in the powerful Gulf Stream current? Some of our colleagues joked that the *Alligator* could have floated all the way to England!

The *Alligator*, however, cannot be considered a submarine as we know them today. It was an 1862 submarine constructed with the materials and methods of the time. Based on the plans in our possession, *Alligator* had many openings in the hull through which water could leak, especially after her re-fit in the Washington Naval Yard before being towed south. President Abraham Lincoln is believed to have witnessed the *Alligator*'s sea trials on the Anacostia River during this re-fit period[11]. The pounding the *Alligator* took in the 1863 storm, and during the tow, most likely filled her with water. But how much, and how quickly?

Studies now began into how the submarine worked, demonstrating how sophisticated it was for the time[12]. Research revealed that when the *Alligator* was re-fitted at the Washington Naval Yard in October 1862, the oars originally placed at 18 stations and used to propel the boat were removed, and the openings through the hull were sealed with gaskets. Replacing the oars, a propeller shaft thru the hull was added for propulsion, also sealed with gaskets. The plans further revealed that 21 portholes ran along the top of the *Alligator*'s 47-foot length. These were fitted into her top with glass "bull's eyes" for light and a lookout observation hatch. All of these features were potential points of leakage. A "lock-out chamber," through which a diver could exit the boat under water to plant mines, presented yet another point of leakage. All in all, there were many places where water could enter the hull during the tow and storm, which buffeted both the *Sumpter* and *Alligator* with 18- to 20-foot seas, never mind leakage from the riveted hull itself.

To help better understand how these openings might leak or fail, Bruce Terrell investigated the gasket materials and construction methods of the time. It was a tough piece of detective work. We concluded the *Alligator* had, indeed, been leaking, possibly heavily, which caused her to fill with water. Some of the correspondence discovered implies the *Alligator* could easily have been leaking when she left the dock in Norfolk – before going under tow into the open seas of the Atlantic. But we couldn't determine how much water and at what rate of entry. Given the plans, however, we could approximate how

---

11 See Appendix F.
12 See Appendix E.

much water within the hull would make the submarine negative, causing her to sink. Then we worked backward and put several possibilities of how fast water may have been entering the hull into modeling scenarios.

We had done some good work trying to piece together all available information to refine the search area for the *Alligator*. In all honesty, however, the great number of uncertainties and guesses involved led us to establish a very large overall search area. Certainly, the *Alligator* or her remains must lie on the bottom. But it was anyone's guess as to which scenario made the most sense for a search.

In the end, all our clever analysis may have been interesting and fun, but it remains unclear how much it helped in the actual search. Finding the *Alligator* continued to be the equivalent of looking for a needle in a very big haystack. Then events transpired that pushed us into an expedition — and a decision of where to look first.

Unexpected Momentum

The discovery of the plans in Paris immediately generated new opportunities to convey the story of the *Alligator*. For example, we created a well-received USS *Alligator* exhibit at the Navy Submarine League's Annual Symposium in June 2003, and an *Alligator* display was featured at an ONR-sponsored conference at the Reagan Center in Washington, D.C., in August 2003. More than just the "word" was getting out.

I had independently been having periodic lunch meetings with Steve Burns, who at the time was executive vice-president of production and chief science editor of Discovery Networks,

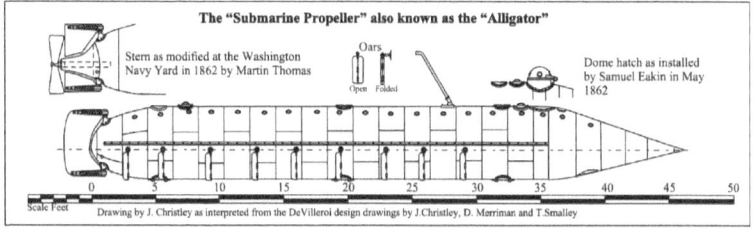

The best interpretative schematic drawing of how the USS *Alligator* was configured for both oar and propeller propulsion.

U.S. Every few months, we would get together to compare notes and ideas. Steve would run by me an interesting film project or two that he was considering, and I would spin him ideas about things we were working on at NOAA, or that were rattling around in the back of my mind. I was certainly the big benefactor of these meetings and the relationship we formed.

Steve still is one of the most experienced directors, producers, and executives in the documentary-film business. He has won more industry awards than almost anyone. He is probably best known for his roles in creating and managing the Discovery Network, U.S., the Discovery Science Channel, and the National Geographic Channels, U.S., and, most recently, as chief programming officer for the Curiosity Stream online channel. Not to mention his work with PBS. I was lucky to meet Steve, and things had just happened. I remember one time I chided him, in a fun way, about the lack of effectiveness of ocean-related documentary films. Steve, always the gentleman, would gently let me know when we didn't necessarily agree on a point or two. In fact, he had made or been involved in well over a hundred such films. I constantly learned about filmmaking from him, and this served me well for decades to come.

It was at one of our lunches, soon after Catherine returned from Paris, that I mentioned the extraordinary find of the plans for the mysterious *Alligator*. Steve's fertile mind immediately began connecting the dots to a potential documentary film, and he said, "What an unbelievable story that would make!" Steve knew just the person to make such a film, and asked if it would be okay if he spoke to him about it? Well, it was more than okay with me. Steve, of course, knew a host of filmmakers and even had a little money to put toward the film project. Over the years, I learned of Steve's great interest in the underwater world — especially submarines. The elements required to make an interesting film would change everything about the search for the USS *Alligator* and push us out to sea before we were ready.

Chapter 7
A Film Changes Everything

Looking back at the events that emerged around the *Alligator*, I am reminded of the age-old conundrum: Which came first, the chicken or the egg? Did our research propel the film, or did the film propel the research? The fact is the requirements of making an interesting film prompted us, in large measure, to learn more about the details of USS *Alligator*'s sophistication and to initiate the first expedition.

Not long after one of my lunches with Steve Burns, he contacted filmmaker and producer Dave Clark to meet and discuss the possibilities of making a film about the *Alligator* story. Steve and Dave had worked together before, and Steve sensed that Dave was perfect for creating and producing the film. Dave was also familiar with the Maritime Heritage Program we were developing at NOAA. He had recently produced a film for the Discovery Science Channel, *The Wreck of the Portland*, about one of our program's first, highly publicized, shipwreck discoveries. Dave is a well-known and award-winning producer, director, and writer specializing in documentaries and non-fiction television programs about natural history, science, and adventure. Having a filmmaker of his caliber on the *Alligator* project was a pleasant surprise.

Poster advertising the release of the Dave Clark's film.

Initially, Dave was uncertain about taking on a film project with so many loose ends. How could he tell an interesting story about a hunt to find a lost submarine about which so little was known and which might never be found? Fortunately, Catherine Marzin's discovery of the *Alligator* plans in Paris provided a compelling aspect upon which he could build the film, and it was a good place to start. That was the easy part because, interesting story or not, a Discovery Science film must include science. Thus, Dave learned as much as he could about the *Alligator* and Brutus de Villeroi to determine what he might be able to "create" that would make the film interesting and also fulfill the science requirement. This led him to undertake efforts and to build storylines that we hadn't yet thought of. I suppose he believed we were further along in our research and understanding. Whatever the case, his filmmaking needs drove our efforts in several directions. I don't recollect the exact order in which they occurred, but they ultimately changed everything.

First Symposium

Overall, interest in the *Alligator* accelerated the summer after we discovered de Villeroi's plans. It was time to assemble everything we knew about the inventor and his invention and present it to as many interested parties as possible. Consequently, the first symposium on the USS *Alligator* convened in October 2003 at the Submarine Force Museum in Groton, Connecticut. It was the ideal place to bring the USS *Alligator* back to life. Tied-up at the museum is the U.S. Navy's first nuclear submarine — the USS *Nautilus*; and here we were,

Left to right: Bob Ballard, RADM Jay Cohen, the author, and Capt. Craig McLean at the First Symposium.

convened to discuss the merits of the U.S. Navy's first submarine — also the most advanced of all that came before it and for its time. RADM Cohen had no doubt "put in the word" to secure the museum. The symposium was akin to a "coming out party" for the *Alligator* after 140 years of obscurity. It also signified how far we had come since that day in the South Pacific aboard the *Sea Scout*, less than 18 months before.

Navy, NOAA, and Team *Alligator* members sent invitations to about 200 potential attendees, and many participated. The symposium brought together: naval historians, marine archeologists, resource managers, oceanographers, artists, documentary filmmakers, maritime museum executives, educators, and other interested parties. Even descendants of Samuel Eakins, who had been intimately involved with the *Alligator* during its short life, attended. As did Alexandre Duplaix from the Service Historique de la Marine, who had brought Catherine the box with de Villeroi's name on it. Duplaix also presented a copy of de Villeroi's original plans to the museum. By the time the symposium ended, Brutus de Villeroi and his invention had, indeed, been re-discovered; and the momentum to find the *Alligator* reached an all-time high. Still, we could not articulate a plan to find it. It was one thing to have a symposium but quite another to bring together the means for a search.

Filming Prompts an Expedition

While the NOAA Ship *Thomas Jefferson* initially made an impromptu cruise to search for the *Alligator* the previous June, I don't refer to that event as the first expedition. The expeditions that followed were far more involved and comprised of many more elements. The actual first expedition evolved to

A converted Army Corps of Engineers' T-boat.

The U.S. Navy's YP-679.

support the needs of the film as well as several other science endeavors prompted by the film.

Following the symposium, Dave Clark continued to formulate the segments he might include in the film. He concluded that the science of searching the seabed was important, and that meant filming actual sequences at sea. At first, this seemed a difficult request to fulfill. But after we discussed the specifics of what Dave had in mind; we determined that a full-blown expedition was unnecessary. Good thing, because we had no means to conduct one. Dave actually needed film sequences shot on a vessel at sea with the appropriate technology — so it gave the appearance of being part of a search. At the time, we didn't even have an appropriate vessel to use. The National Marine Sanctuaries' vessel-building program was just getting underway; and we had yet to acquire our own tools of the trade — magnetometers, side-scan sonars, and remotely operated vehicles (ROVs). Eventually, the vessels would be built and equipped with the right technology, but that was all in the future.

Tim Runyan, a professor of marine archeology at East Carolina University, came to NOAA on an annual basis to assist me in developing our Maritime Heritage Program. Not only was Tim a well-known leader in marine archeology and museums, but, as a professor, he had trained a cadre of practicing marine archeologists around the country. Eventually, I hired many of his former students to work in the fledgling program. I was fortunate to have Tim working with me, particularly at this time. We discussed the conundrum of finding a way to satisfy Dave Clark's need for at-sea sequences, and Tim rose to the occasion as usual.

East Carolina University owned an old Army Corps of Engineers vessel, a T-boat, that they used for marine studies that we might be able to use. We also had some experiences with T-boats. They are about 60 feet in length and not necessarily made for operations out to sea, but this one would work for the film's purposes. The university's marine archeology program also had a magnetometer and side-scan sonar, which they would loan to us. But it got even better. The program had just purchased an ROV — the NOVA Ray — from a company in California. As ROVs go, it was capable for our purposes and could be launched easily off the side of a vessel. No one at the university had yet used the NOVA Ray, and I got the impression it was still being field tested by the company. But it would do. If Tim could arrange with the university to use the T-boat and the necessary equipment — and we could afford it. We had a way to film the segments at sea.

These developments delighted RADM Cohen. One day at lunch, as we discussed how to maximize this opportunity, we concluded the operation should also survey part of the *Alligator* search area. After all, the appropriate equipment would be on board. Then I saw a gleam in RADM Cohen's eyes. I had seen this before and knew his brain had just connected the dots. "Why don't we use my research demonstration vessel, the YP-679? It's already set up for things like this and has a great control room space. It's also much larger, 108 feet, and we can do a lot more with it by bringing other related projects aboard at the same time." Then, with an even brighter glow in his eyes, he added, "It'll be free, and I will provide the crew. What a deal — right?" We both laughed. The die was cast. Dave Clark's desire to film a segment at sea led to a joint Navy/NOAA expedition. It became a major, multi-day event held in the little town of Ocracoke on the Outer Banks along North Carolina's coast. As it turned out, Dave got his film footage, but unexpected events intervened, and the expedition suddenly got very real[13].

---

13 The following chapter describes the Ocracoke events and what occurred at sea on board the YP-679 in 2004.

Jules Verne and the Alligator

The discovery of de Villeroi's plans in Paris was colossal. The Discovery Channel sent Catherine and a film crew to Paris to reenact the event. The footage was important to the film, but something had also been added: A visit to the Jules Verne Institute. There was speculation that the submarine *Nautilus* in Jules Verne's classic novel, *Twenty Thousand Leagues Under the Sea*, was copied from de Villeroi's *Alligator* design. There was an uncanny similarity between them, especially the lock-out chamber that allowed divers to exit the craft and walk on the seabed. Jules Verne is not known to have built or designed a submarine, and nothing is written about an association between the two men. The visit to the institute, however, provided additional circumstantial information and helped clarify the speculation about the vessels.

Both Brutus de Villeroi and Jules Verne hailed from the city of Nantes on the Loire River in Brittany. Early in his career, de Villeroi taught mathematics in the local schools where Jules Verne was a student. Jules Verne would have been very young at this time. There are, however, no records to indicate de Villeroi taught any classes that Jules Verne attended. But de Villeroi was widely known in Nantes and the Loire region, and flattering articles about his inventions often appeared in local newspapers as well as magazines in Paris. In the early 1830s, he was testing submarine designs in the waters at the mouth of the Loire River, downstream from Nantes. But, at this time, de Villeroi was not the only Frenchman experimenting with submarine designs and ideas, including the concept of lock-out chambers. Other inventors were also likely in the news. But it stands to reason that an interested and inquiring mind, such as possessed by the young Jules Verne, at least knew of de Villeroi and his inventions. Nonetheless, we found no "new" evidence at the Jules Verne Institute to corroborate a relationship between de Villeroi and Jules Verne. For fans of the Jules Verne classic, the inspiration for the *Nautilus* remains a mystery.

Navy Science

De Villeroi's plans illustrate, and his correspondence mentions, an air-purification device to refresh the air in the *Alligator*, extending its time underwater. No detailed explanation of how the device worked is known. But concepts using *lime*, calcium oxide, derived from natural limestone for such purposes appear as far back as the 1830s. It was, however, a science question as to how de Villeroi's device may have worked, and if, in fact, it could have purified or refreshed the air in the submarine. As a long-time Navy submariner, RADM Cohen knew exactly where and to whom to bring the problem. He and Dave Clark took this question to the Naval Submarine Medical Research Laboratory (NSMRL) in Groton.

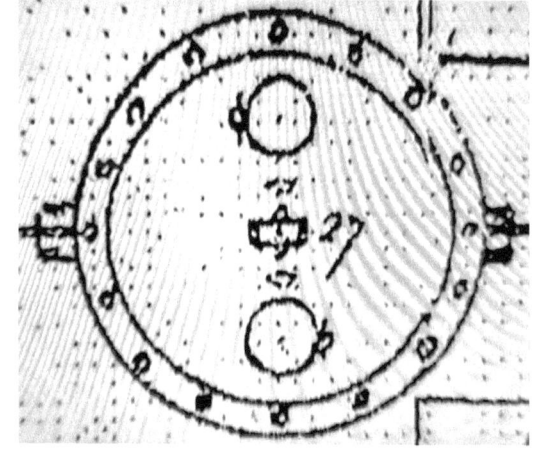

Air-purification device from de Villeroi's plans.

The NSMRL's research became an interesting science segment in the film. It compared de Villeroi's approach to refreshing air in his submarine to roughly analogous methods the U.S. Navy uses under certain circumstances today. From de Villeroi's plans, Navy researchers calculated the volume of air in the *Alligator*; and then, given the number of crew members within the hull, they calculated the time it would take for the carbon dioxide (CO_2) inside the submarine to reach a dangerous level. In one correspondence, de Villeroi indicated this would take approximately four hours. The U.S. Navy researchers estimated it would be considerably less. Whatever the estimate, it is clear that de Villeroi knew he had to reduce the CO_2 generated inside the hull to increase the amount of time the *Alligator* could stay submerged.

De Villeroi's plans show a system that somehow forced the air in the submarine through a device that somehow purified it. In today's closed-circuit diving systems worn by scuba divers, aptly named re-breathers, air is forced through a canister filled with a CO_2-absorbing material, thus removing the CO_2 a diver breathes and dramatically extending the time a diver can stay submerged. De Villeroi's idea was pretty much the same, but could it work?

Navy researchers concluded that de Villeroi's device most likely used lime, which was a well-known and readily available compound, as a purifier. They conducted experiments bubbling CO_2 gas through a tank filled with water and crushed limestone to determine if CO_2 gas could be removed — and it worked. This may, indeed, be the method de Villeroi contemplated using in his device. Nonetheless, no engineering specifications exist for de Villeroi's device as to limestone concentrations, air-flow rates, or effectiveness. But now the facts were clear: The *Alligator* featured advanced air purification, which could have worked. It was yet another example of the technological advances de Villeroi incorporated into his invention. While Dave Clark captured an interesting segment for the film, we corroborated more of the *Alligator*'s secrets.

Navy Tests the Alligator

We know the *Alligator* endured a shakedown cruise in the Anacostia River, after her re-fit with a "propeller" and new rudder in the Washington Naval Yard, and that she worked to satisfaction. But it was 1863, and people didn't know much about submarines or how they should perform. Now, after almost 150 years of innovation and experience, naval architects and submarine designers questioned the *Alligator*'s seaworthiness. There was only one way to answer this question: build a working-scale model and test it.

In Dave Clark's continuing efforts to develop segments for the film, he discovered that a couple of model builders were constructing an operating 1:12 scale model of the USS *Alligator*. The model was based on de Villeroi's original plans, which we had made public. It turned out that an entire community of professional model builders work in the background, crafting models of historic ships, aircraft, vehicles, etc. What's more, the Navy, others in the military, and the private sector engage the modelers to "mock-up," or build, scale models of new designs and concepts. For our purposes, Dave Clark had found the key to understanding the *Alligator* as a submarine. Sure, he would get some spectacular footage, but the world would finally know if the 1862 *Alligator* had really worked.

Discovery paid for model builders to take their working model of the *Alligator* to the U.S. Navy's premier test facility at

The U.S. Navy's premier test facility at Carderock, Maryland.

Carderock, Maryland, for an evaluation. The Navy agreed to place the *Alligator* model into its world-class, instrumented test tank to evaluate its performance, as it does for every ship or submarine built for the U.S. Navy. This unbelievable *coup* was possible only because some in the Navy now had serious interest in the USS *Alligator*. And featuring the prestigious but not well-publicized naval facility in a film was good for the Navy.

In the fall of 2004, model makers David Merriman and Tim Smalley brought their *Alligator* model to the David Taylor Test Basin within the Carderock facility. In this version, the oars were replaced by a propeller. Hence, the model could actually be operated in the test tank. Accompanying them were the Discovery film team, including underwater videographer, my old friend, Nick Caloyianis, who filmed the *Alligator* model as it maneuvered underwater in the test tank, as well as interested Navy and NOAA personnel.

A diver prepares a working scale-model of the *Alligator* for the test tank at Carderock.

Jim Christley's painting of how the Alligator might have looked during an operation.

The experts at the test tank wanted to answer a number of specific questions. No one had ever seen or tested a submarine like the *Alligator*. It was a first. Its long hull with no apparent control surfaces, as are present on modern submarines, raised the question about the stability and controllability of the hull when moving underwater. It might be impossible to control at all. The shape of the stern and rudders underscored this concern. They were not exactly the way today's naval architects design them. How would de Villeroi's submarine turn and maneuver? Would it be the nimble weapon of war he claimed?

Also there was the big question of how the *Alligator* adjusted its buoyancy. The two "buoyancy cylinders" in de Villeroi's plans were designed to be let out of and pulled back into the submarine by cables to help control the submarine's buoyance underwater. How would this work, especially when underway? No one had ever seen or heard of such a setup. There was now a lot of interest in what de Villeroi, the self-anointed genius, had designed and sold to the U.S. Navy.

In 1862, people thought of submarine operations very differently than they do today. They had no choice. None of the features or technology now associated with submarines had been invented — not even the periscope. The technology and understanding of submarines in war was in its infancy. Consequently, the *Alligator* was designed to travel just beneath the surface in shallow water, although de Villeroi made extreme claims as to its capability to reach great depths. How else could divers be placed on the seabed where they would attach explosive mines to ships or to obstacles blocking channels? No matter what marvelous new inventions de Villeroi incorporated into the *Alligator*, the submarine could operate within a very limited envelope. The testing at Carderock considered this reality. For me, the question was: Could the *Alligator* perform the tasks and mission(s) for which it was being towed to Savanah and Charleston, before being cut loose and sinking from the pages of history?

Watching the tests was fascinating. Just being in the facility was impressive; the technology and tools of naval architecture were displayed everywhere. I thought of all the Naval vessels that began their journeys in those tanks and on those test stands. Dave Clark hit a home run as far as the film was concerned. The experts agreed that de Villeroi had got it just about right. As it turned out, the *Alligator* was stable as a rock underway, especially when those odd buoyancy cylinders were extended, and she could almost turn within her length. Since she could never travel very fast — a hand-crank turned the propeller — the cylinders never would have presented a problem underway. Yes, de Villeroi had gotten it mostly right, according to today's experts!

None of this would have occurred except for the need to make an interesting film, and neither would the first expedition proceed when and how it did. Making a film changed everything and dramatically drove forward the knowledge of the *Alligator* and public interest in it. The next several years were marked by our attempts to find this iconic lost submarine — all of them propelled forward by the making of a film. As for de Villeroi and his invention? Maybe he had a claim to be a genius, after all.

Chapter 8

Expedition to Ocracoke

As we started planning to find the USS *Alligator*, the full scope of possibilities for what we could achieve became clear. Given the specially fitted YP-679, we could conduct an actual expedition in search of the long-lost Civil War submarine; and Dave Clark could easily get his film sequences at sea. While it was unlikely we would find the *Alligator*, we could also make progress on our Maritime Heritage Program agenda. In fact, the search created attention and interest that allowed us to move forward in many other areas, including developing STEM education programs based on the *Alligator*; attracting additional qualified staff, forming relationships with new partners in industry, academia, and museums; and, not to be underestimated, enhancing our stature within the agency, the government in general, and even on Capitol Hill. Such was the powerful draw of a hunt for the *Alligator*. Consequently, we began organizing an effort far greater than just running survey lines and getting Dave's footage for the film.

We planned operations for a week at sea, covering a search area seaward of Cape Hatteras, and we needed an appropriate port or anchorage from which to deploy the YP-679. The docks at the small town of Ocracoke, on the bay side of Ocracoke Island and part of North Carolina's Outer Banks, comprised the closest port able to support the expedition's goals. Ocracoke is not the easiest place to access. Vehicles are ferried across the

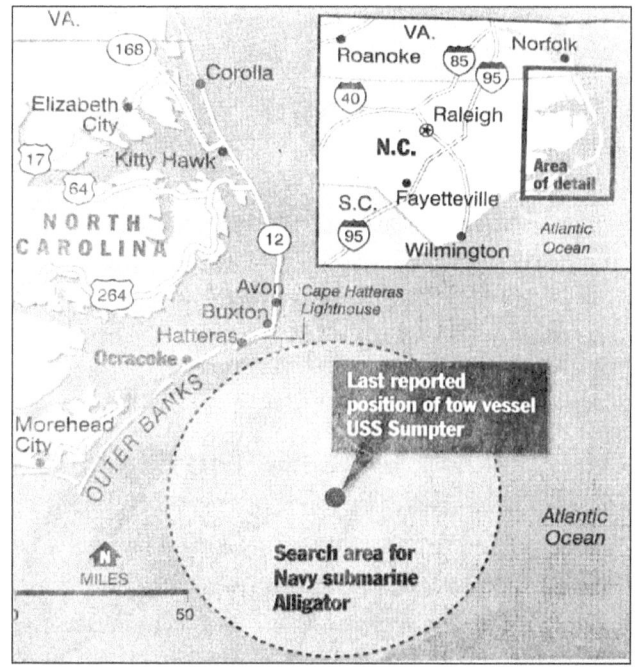

Chart showing both Okracoke Island, part of North Carolina's Outer Banks, and the last reported position of the USS *Sumpter*.

Hatteras Inlet to Ocracoke Island, and the YP-679 had to navigate the shallow Ocracoke Inlet, mindful of the tides. Even so, Ocracoke was perfect. A well-known iconic village, Ocracoke draws tourists from around the world. What's more, a U.S. Navy vessel hadn't visited there since World War II. Thus, the YP-679's arrival was an attraction in itself that would resonate throughout the Outer Banks. It was a great location and venue for creating events and presenting the expedition and our messages to a large, interested audience.

Aboard the YP-679, we planned to survey the search area using the equipment setup Tim Runyon orchestrated with East Carolina University. But what started as a simple "ask" by

Dave Clark to get a little at-sea footage quickly became a large, multi-pronged operation. Thanks to the YP-679's special configuration, we brought other programs, staff, scientists, educators, and observers aboard each day. Mike Overfield, whom I made the expedition's chief scientist, designed an excellent survey plan. The survey got underway as a proverbial "shot in the dark" until an unsolicited phone call on the third day at Ocracoke changed everything. The call would impact the hunt for the *Alligator* for the next two years.

Mike Overfield got involved with Team *Alligator* early in 2002 during conversations with Bruce Terrell. He was Catherine's office contact when she discovered Brutus de Villeroi's plans in Paris. Even without an assignment, Mike immediately focused his creative mind toward finding the *Alligator*. The whole story captivated him, and, as he would later say, "The *Alligator* story is exactly why I had gotten into marine archeology." Mike's undergraduate degree was in history, but he was initially lured into the business world. It was too much for him to resist, and he was good at it. But he dreamed of becoming a marine archeologist, and his passion eventually won out. When he was in his early forties, he dropped his business career and entered the Marine Archeology Graduate Program at East Carolina University (ECU). The same qualities that made him successful in business helped him to become what I consider a unique archeologist. He was incredibly open to new ideas and brought an entirely different perspective to projects. I think a lot of people in the organization watched him closely to learn from him.

Before assigning Mike to be chief scientist aboard the YP-679, I talked it over with Tim Runyan, who had been Mike's advisor at ECU and knew him well. Tim gave me a big smile, almost laughing. "Oh yeah," he said. "Mike's the guy. He will do more than just pull this expedition off — trust me." I did, and the rest is history. Mike headed the challenge to find the *Alligator*, leading the 2005 and 2006 expeditions as well.

Ocracoke

Preparing to operate out of Ocracoke and to bring attention to the expedition required serious planning. The August expedition was big news up and down the Outer Banks in the summer of 2004. David Hall, a public affairs officer from NOAA, and others drew attention to the *Alligator* story and publicized the upcoming expedition. On June 4, the weekend edition of the *Virginia Pilot* published an excellent *Alligator* article featuring an artist's depiction of the submarine with comparative facts and information. This rendition remains the best single-page summary of the *Alligator*[14].

On August 22, the YP-679 began its week-long stay at Ocracoke, docked at the National Park Service docks next to Silver Lake Harbor and the Ocracoke Preservation Museum. This location was excellent for YP-679 operations and public events. With the cooperation of the harbor and museum, a large tent was pitched and fitted with chairs, a podium, sound system, and large screen for slide presentations. On Tuesday, August 24, the third day of the expedition, we held a public event under the tent and on the docks. Among the speakers, Catherine was the star. Attendees were fascinated by her Paris discovery and wanted to hear the details from Catherine herself.

RADM Jay Deloach spoke for the U.S. Navy. Jay was a Naval reserve officer and reserve deputy commander with

---

14 See part of this article in Chapter 2, "The *Alligator*'s Place Among Early Submarines."

the Submarine Force, U.S. Atlantic Fleet. When RADM Cohen originally told Jay Deloach about the *Alligator*, he came to see me. We spoke several times before the events at Ocracoke. Jay Deloach is, by nature, a history buff. He immediately got involved with the *Alligator* and it remains a passion of his. A protégé of RDAM Cohen, RDAM Deloach possessed lots of Navy-submarine experience, and the *Alligator* story fit squarely in his "wheelhouse." Another speaker, Craig McLean, who was then a captain, represented NOAA's Office of Ocean Exploration. Craig would go on to higher roles in NOAA. Members of the Ocracoke community also spoke. I might have said a word or two. Dave Clark and his team filmed much of the event, as did David Hall. The well-attended event drew people from up and down the Outer Banks and off-island. The Hatteras Ferry had a busy day.

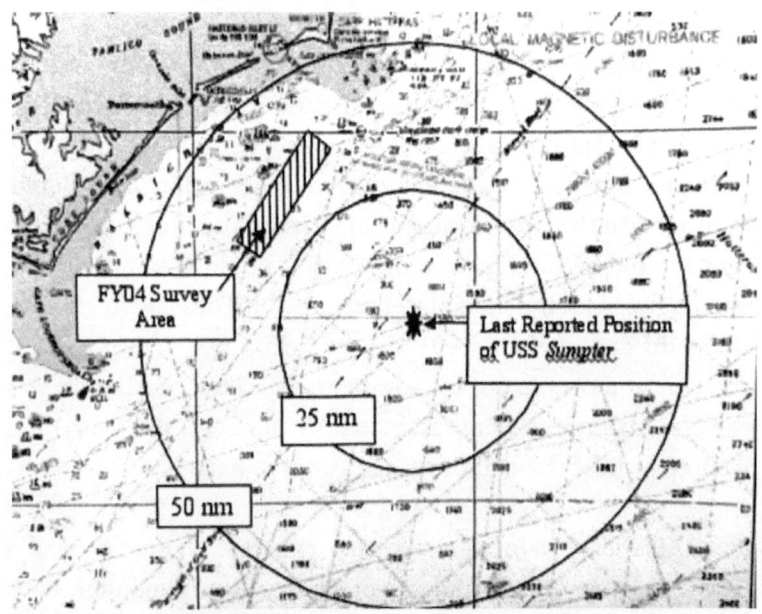

Chart with the last reported position of the USS *Sumpter* and the planned survey area for the USS *Alligator*.

Following the presentations, the YP-679 was available for public and media tours. Mike Overfield and his science party led visitors and members of the media through the control room and explained how the magnetometer, towed side-scan sonar, and ROV worked, and how each computer monitor fit into operations. The Navy crew did the rest. Mike was especially popular with the media as he weaved the science of exploration into the *Alligator*'s historical significance and made clear to all the value of maritime heritage. Like Tim Runyan said, Mike would do so much more — and he did. But, before this day was over, an unsolicited phone call to Craig McLean from a treasure salvor — part of a group that is unpopular with marine archeologists and historians — changed the trajectory of this expedition and of the expeditions to come.

Anonymous Target

The first days aboard the YP-679 were dedicated to getting equipment aboard, determining how the towed equipment would be launched and recovered, configuring the control room, and integrating the digital survey lines into the on-board navigation system of the ship. The YP-679 was a very capable ship; it was, after all, an ONR demonstration-and-test platform. The T-boat we originally planned to use was not even comparable. Thus, the YP-679 took to sea, enabling us to test equipment, while Dave Clark got most of his footage, including segments of Mike and the science party running a few survey lines. But, as we soon learned, a peculiarity of the YP-679's modification for training at the Naval Academy would pose a problem.

We sent some NOAA divers along to help Dave Clark and his team get the so-called "money shots" of the gear entering the water and moving underwater. In past projects, I had been in the water getting these types of shots, and so I knew exactly what the divers and cameramen were doing. The number one shot is the ROV as it breaks the surface and descends past the camera. Later, when the YP-679 tied up at the National Park Service docks for the open house, we had plenty of footage to show and tell the visitors.

I never asked Craig how he knew the treasurer salvor who called that afternoon. Both Craig and I had dived a lot of shipwrecks, and, as part of the shipwreck-diving community, we came across myriad "treasurer seekers." But I didn't know the individual who called Craig. The treasure salvor and his colleagues had read the *Virginia Pilot* article about the *Alligator* and thought they could help us.

For at least the last decade, they had worked off of the East Coast, lowering "drop cameras" to look for possible treasures. In 1986, they passed through the approximate area where the *Alligator* was cut loose. Their method of discovery was to navigate around and drop a video camera on so-called "bumps" of interest on the bottom. They used a weighted video camera in a waterproof housing, attached to a line, and suspended just above the bottom over the target bump. They claimed they had seen something that might be of interest to us. It was not what they were looking for and they simply moved on. They said they had videotape that showed something like a boiler with a port hole and what looked like a large propeller.

This was dramatic news. Craig quickly found me on board the YP-679. He was excited and looked like someone who had a secret to tell. "Dano," he said. "You aren't going to believe the call I just got!" We moved to a private corner on the portbridge wing to discuss the phone call. Could we possibly be so lucky? Had these treasure salvors accidentally stumbled upon the *Alligator*'s remains? It was clear we needed to get a look at the videotape. Craig got back to them and asked them to immediately send us a copy and any relevant position information. The tape that arrived was a grainy, probably third-generation VHS or Beta tape. I wasn't quite sure I could see what they saw on the tape. But others looked and imagined they could see something. Even many months later, in the quiet of our offices, I could not make out much on that tape. I think the power of suggestion is real; individuals will sometimes imagine they see things they want to see. Nevertheless, we now had a "real target" to investigate and resolve — one way or the other. Was it the remains of the *Alligator* or something else? Perhaps it was simply a pile of junk on the bottom.

The first couple of days aboard the YP-679 were lighthearted. Everyone knew the real purpose of our expedition was to provide Dave Clark with the scenes he needed for the film and to do a little surveying along the way. But that phone call changed everything, and the tenor on board the YP-679 the next day became very different. Craig and I, consulting with RADM Jay Deloach and Mike Overfield, decided to redirect the YP-679 and search operations to the new target area once we had a better fix on its position. The hunt for the *Alligator* was now real. So if tomorrow was the real thing — and, through an unforeseen coincidence, the remains of the *Alligator* were waiting for us to find them — I thought it was important for certain individuals, in addition to Mike and members of the science party, to be on the YP-679.

I pressured Jay Deloach to come aboard the YP-679 the following day, even though I knew he suffered from motion sickness. In fact, he often joked that motion sickness was one reason he went into the submarine service — stable platforms. I think I guilted him into going. "Don't you want to be on board and bear witness to the discovery of the U.S. Navy's lost

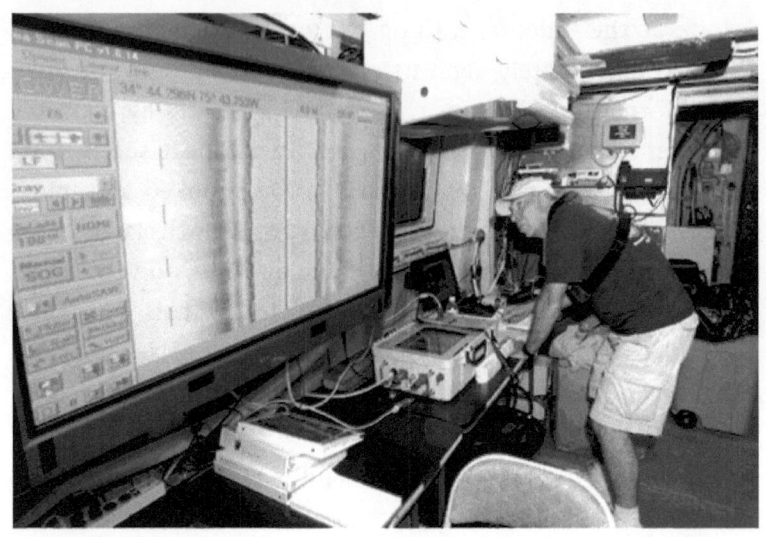

Mike Overfield checks the side-scan sonar monitor in the control room.

first submarine?" I asked. Motion sickness is truly unpleasant. I have endured it twice in my career and wouldn't wish it on anyone. But this could be the big day. Jay gave me a crooked smile, knowing what he was getting into. RADM Jay Deloach was on the YP-679 the next day. Others on board included Tom Nutter, science advisor at ONR, representing RADM Cohen; Tim Runyan; Dwight Coleman; Dave Clark; John Broadwater, the superintendent of USS *Monitor* National Marine Sanctuary; and others. Mike Overfield made sure the entire science party, including the ROV contractor's technicians, were on board the next day for the morning muster and briefing. I was pleased Dwight Coleman came down from Rhode Island to join us. Dwight worked closely with Bob Ballard on his discovery expeditions, and I had seen Dwight in action on at least three of them. Dwight was the most experienced scientist in underwater-search techniques and analysis on board the YP-679 that day. Catherine and Michiko were also on board to bear witness, if we actually found the

Alligator. They also videotaped interviews and scenes for the STEM education program they were developing about the science behind the "Hunt for the *Alligator*." The weather forecast for the following day was mostly sunny with light breezes, and the sea state seemed pretty normal for Cape Hatteras. But what's actually predictable about the seas off of Cape Hatteras is that they are unpredictable!

The treasure salvors provided us with Loran-C navigation bearings for the location where they had dropped the video camera. The Loran radio-navigation system, developed during World War II, was the primary system that ships used to determine their locations until it was discontinued in 2010. (GPS now makes it easy for anyone with a cell phone to know their position.) Loran-C beacons sighted along the coast were used routinely in 1986 as well as 2004. Shipwreck hunters and salvors coveted their Loran bearings, or numbers, for the shipwrecks they valued. How else could shipwrecks, once found, be revisited when they were far out to sea and not visible from land? The downside is that a position plotted on a nautical chart using the Loran receiver on the vessel is accurate only for the chart used. Use the same chart to plot the position and all is well. Change to a chart with a different datum and the position is off. We had no idea on which chart and datum the treasure salvor's bearings were based. Therefore, two positions of the target were plotted with different chart datums, and a "box" drawn around them. The distance between the plots was in the order of hundreds of feet. When we went to sea the next day, we would not survey along Mike Overfield's original survey lines. The plan now was to go directly to the new box area and run the magnetometer and side-scan sonar along new lines in the small box. If a promising target were found, we would put the ROV on it. Interestingly, the new box was within the larger block Mike had laid out to survey. The next day was the real thing.

Hunt Is On

Dawn came bright and sunny with a light breeze. The day started with an early muster aboard the YP-679. Once all were aboard, the crew, science party, and everyone else convened in the control room. This was the first time most of them would hear about the treasure salvor's phone call and learn that today was the real thing. I personally addressed the control room, explained everything, and swore everyone to secrecy. If it became known that we had a promising position, others would attempt to shadow us, getting a fix on our position and maybe the *Alligator*. The Outer Banks population knew we were in Ocracoke and what we were doing. Many watched the YP-679 go out of the inlet during the previous days or saw it offshore. If we found the *Alligator*, there was little we could do to protect it from treasure salvors once we left the site.

The looting of shipwrecks is a serious problem. In the following years, I confronted it at least a half-dozen times on noteworthy shipwrecks. Indeed, on the remainder of this expedition, the YP-679 played "cat and mouse" with various other vessels out at sea. During the briefing, I clarified the YP-679's chain of command. There were new people on board and not everyone was familiar with who was in charge and how things worked. But today was the real thing and everyone had to be clear. Things at sea often don't work out as planned, and who makes the calls becomes critical. Once we passed out of the inlet, Mike Overfield, as chief scientist, was in total charge of every aspect of the survey; the ship's captain was responsible for everything else. Other senior individuals on board, including myself, would act only as advisors. Leaving the inlet, I could not have imagined all the things that were about to go wrong. It turned out that a lot of collaborative head-scratching took place throughout the day as we tried to overcome the unforeseen problems that kept coming up.

As the YP-679 moved into the sea, I went forward to sun myself, relax on the front deck, and enjoy the three-hour cruise to the box. I had experienced many such cruises in these waters and usually enjoyed the trip out. I wasn't there long when RADM Jay Deloach came by and told me he was "getting that feeling" and was going below to the sleeping compartments, the most stable place on the ship. Then it hit me that the only time I had motion sickness was in these very waters off Cape Hatteras. Now I really felt guilty for pressing Jay to come along. I remember thinking we'd better find the *Alligator* today or I might lose a friend. But, as the day progressed, more and more individuals "got the feeling." Jay had lots of company in the sleeping compartments!

Finally, we approached the new box. Mike assembled the science party on the rear deck, ready to go. Mike's plan was first to tow the magnetometer along the survey lines, then the side-scan sonar. There were many hands at work, preparing the units, getting them overboard, setting up the tow line, and then, in the control room, monitoring and acquiring the data. Graduate students from ECU and NOAA personnel performed most of these tasks under Mike's hands-on supervision. He knew almost everyone. Tim Runyan was particularly helpful on the back deck, and Dwight Clark remained in the control room, keeping his experienced eye on the activity. A genuine sense of excitement filled the air. Dave Clark could film anything he wanted but had to stay in the background as an observer. For me, it was fun just to be a part of it.

Serious Setbacks

The search box was pretty small, and it didn't take long to tow gear down one line and then back on another. As I recall, the first hint of a problem occurred when I walked into the control room to watch the side-scan sonar returns on a large monitor. The real-time sonar images were showing a perfectly flat bottom with no disturbance of any kind. It was too neat; I had seen this before. I spoke with a few others observing the images, but it didn't seem to bother them. I grabbed Dwight and Mike to come and look. I said: "This looks to me like the side-scan is too high off the bottom and not able to pick it up." Mike and Dwight looked at the images and said: "You might be right. We have to get it lower."

To acquire good sonar images, the sonar unit must be towed or driven at a prescribed altitude above the bottom. Clearly, we weren't doing that. There are only two ways to get a towed unit closer to the bottom: attach a depressor weight to the tow line or slow down the boat and the tow. A depressor weight pulls the tow line directly downward from the towing vessel, which straightens the line above the weight and allows the towed unit at the end of the line to get closer to the bottom. Change the position of the weight along the line and the angles change, and adjustments can be made. I asked Mike: "How about we adjust the depressor?" Mike responded: "There isn't any." Then it struck me that most ECU marine archeology projects took place in shallower waters — rivers and lakes — and not in the open ocean with all its challenges and depth. We were operating at depths of around 200 feet or more. The ECU archeologists probably didn't use depressor weights often and could just slow down their small boat enough to get close to the bottom. Hence, no depressor weights were attached to the line or brought aboard the YP-679.

Our only option was to slow the YP-679 well below 4 knots to around 2 knots. That might get the side-scan sonar near enough to the bottom. We could always speed up and increase the altitude if it got too close. Mike and I went to the bridge to huddle with the captain. The key question was: How slow could we go and still maintain our course on the survey lines? The open-ocean variables — the swell, currents, and winds — can easily move a vessel off course. Even veering 25 feet off course can make the difference between finding something or not. We decided to experiment, and the captain slowed the YP-679 while we monitored the sonar images. At 2 knots, the vessel waddled off course, and the captain could not easily get back on course and hold it. The YP-679 was steering in S-turns along the survey lines. To make matters worse, the side-scan unit was still too far off the bottom. Things weren't going well, but we remained optimistic.

The YP-679 had been a training ship at the Naval Academy. She was not designed to be a survey vessel. What's more, she had been modified at the Naval Academy, fitted with small rudders so that midshipmen could get the feel of a larger, more sluggish ship like the ones on which they might eventually serve. When the academy declared the YP-679 as surplus, RADM Cohen picked her up for ONR and refitted her. But the rudders remained the same. The captain was aware of the modified rudders and had been unsure of how slow he could go and maintain a precise course. He knew now, and so did we. Without a depressor, the side-scan survey was out. But the captain was monitoring his fathometer, and it showed a slight rise or bump off the bottom — smack in the box we had gone over.

The fathometer also showed a congregation of fish hovering above the bump. Of course, the sonar had shown nothing. Fish often congregate on shipwrecks. The slightly elevated rubble remaining on the bottom provides habitat or related food sources for fish. Some of us had seen this many times. Mike and I looked at each other, breathed a sigh of relief, and concluded that it was a real target. Always pragmatic, Mike was ready to abandon the side-scan sonar survey plan. "We have a good target," he said. "Let's just focus on it, drop the ROV on it, and go for it." The captain was confident that the YP-679 could loiter around the bump long enough for us to get a good look.

Up came the sonar gear and the contractor's technicians prepared the ROV to enter the water. All the cables and connections were checked, the control room monitors slightly reconfigured, and the video screens and consoles fired up — all was good to go. We thought we had it right, and optimism returned to everyone on board. As the ROV descended through the water column, I stood again in the control room and watched the first video come in. Dwight Coleman stood next to me. All looked good for almost a minute. Then screens went fuzzy and, finally, dark. Dwight uttered, "Oh, I know what that is — watertight seals or connectors are leaking." Yup, it was the dreaded, too-familiar sight on the monitors that no one likes to see. The gear had to come up, and the trouble diagnosed and repaired. Sometimes this takes a while and throws off the plan for an entire day. Fortunately, we had experts, the contractor's technicians, on board. But the technicians were nowhere to be found as we brought the ROV back to the surface. Mike left to search for them.

Mike returned to the control room and looked none too happy. "You are not going to believe this!" he said, clearly annoyed. His happy-go-lucky composure was gone. "They are down below in the sleeping compartments, sick as dogs," he said. "They can't even come on deck." Apparently, they were fighting "that feeling" just as Jay Deloach did when we left the inlet and had lost it. When the YP-679 had stopped to launch the ROV, she wallowed in the swell, which pushed the technicians over the edge, and, once over that edge, there is no coming back. Both technicians were out for the count, and we didn't see them again until we re-entered the inlet that evening. Before we returned, others joined them below. Even though the YP-679 was 108 feet in length, which may seem big to many people, it was a pretty small vessel for ocean use. It takes a lot of energy for a person just to be at sea for an entire day in a small vessel. The body is always working to balance itself, and if an individual isn't used to it, the tiredness, along with excessive motion, is a recipe for motion sickness. Certainly, we wanted the technicians to work on the ROV and others to do their jobs, but this stuff just happens. After all, wasn't this supposed to be a leisurely operation primarily to fulfill Dave Clark's needs?

Before our three-hour transit back to Ocracoke, a squall hit with a heavy downpour and fog. The pelting rain calmed the sea a bit and the YP-679 settled down. Several patients from the sleeping compartments ventured back up to the main deck, but once the squall passed, they quickly retreated below. On the other hand, Michiko and Catherine found this to be the perfect time to shoot video commentary for their STEM education programming. I presumed they thought the rain and fog made for interesting material. As the squall began to fade, we made another slow pass over the target with the depth finder. There was definitely something there.

It was a long, slow ride back to Hatteras Inlet and Ocracoke. There was a sense of disappointment, given the excitement and hope we had when we left the dock early that morning. Still, we were returning with something for our efforts — a target that might be the *Alligator*. There was more to investigate at this location, and what we needed most was the ROV. If we could get back to the site and put the ROV on the target, the mystery could probably be solved. That is, was or wasn't it the remains of the *Alligator*?

The following day, the YP-679 departed early, carrying the repaired ROV. Only the science party was aboard with the primary mission to get the ROV onto the target — the bump on the bottom with the fish congregation above it — and carefully videotape the entire feature. Three hours later, the YP-679 was over the target, and launched the ROV. To the disbelief and dissatisfaction of everyone on board, the screens quickly became fuzzy and dark. This time, the technicians felt well enough to attempt an ROV repair. But, after a short while, it seemed hopeless. The little NOVA RAY was not up to the task. No one fully knew what the problems were, but it wasn't just leaks. We came to find out that the NOVA RAY was brand new and had yet to see much use.

Nonetheless, determined to get "usable" video of the bump, creative minds went to work. The idea was to remove the camera and its housing from the ROV, attach it to a line, and drop it over the target — just as the treasure salvors had in 1986. It was an inspired idea: adapting on the spot to get the job done. Unfortunately, leakage and video-signal interference problems prevailed. When the camera did work, the images it collected were of poor quality and captured only a glimpse of the bottom in the target vicinity. This was the last opportunity on this expedition to resolve a target that could be the remains of the *Alligator*. The YP-679 spent another day or so at sea supporting NOAA's Maritime Heritage Program, but pending weather ended this work early. The Hatteras weather continued to plague our efforts.

The expedition did not find the *Alligator*, but no one really expected it would. What did happen, as a result of the expedition and all the activities surrounding it, is that the USS *Alligator* was now firmly on its journey into the history books. Dave Clark shot far more footage than he anticipated, giving him what he needed to finish the film. For us — RADM Cohen, the Navy, and NOAA — what now? Mike Overfield was soon hatching plots to return to the bump on the bottom off of Hatteras to resolve this target, one way or the other. Thus, the hunt continued on.

Chapter 9
The Hunt Continues

First things first, as always. We needed to resolve the target — the bump on the sea bottom with a congregation of fish above it — before we went much further. Our analysis and modeling of the 1863 storm and of the USS *Alligator* proved one thing: The *Alligator* could have drifted for a long time, driven by the storm and caught up in the powerful Gulf Stream. When it finally sank, it could have broken apart on the way down or when it impacted the bottom. Randomly searching the vast area on the continental shelf, where the *Alligator* might have come to rest, could take years, even if the ships and technology were available. If the *Alligator* drifted beyond the continental shelf before finally sinking, she was likely lost for all time. There was no solid logic or reasoning to search any particular area of the shelf over another. Yes, we originally went to sea primarily to fulfill Dave Clark's filming requirements. The target position provided by the treasure salvor had been serendipitous. But, when things got real, we were caught without the best equipment and, as it turned out, not the best vessel. We did the best we could with what we had; and I think we all felt we might have missed an opportunity. Nonetheless, we still had that target to resolve: Was it the remains of the *Alligator*? Optimistically, Mike Overfield began to plan an expedition for the 2005 field season to do it right and get an answer.

Last Gasp in 2004

Before the 2004 season was over, we gave it one more try with a different approach. With the target and a position confirmed with the fathometer and given my diving background, my reaction was simply to dive the site and see. This was a deep dive — to a little over 200 feet — but it could be done. We'd use a small boat to navigate as close to the target as possible. Then we'd drop over the side a heavy weight attached to a line, which would sink to the bottom, hopefully landing near the target. Divers would descend along the line to the target and search within the vicinity of the "drop weight." When ready to ascend, they would go back the up line. The boat had to be large enough to carry multiple divers with all their tanks and gear — including cameras — and at least 300 feet of heavy line. The boat also had to be equipped with a Loran-C receiver and to be a good ride to 30 miles offshore. It's fair to say that some of the archeologists involved were not fans of this "non-scientific" method to identify the remains, especially with non-archeologists doing the work. But that is another story.

It was suggested that we engage the U.S. Navy Salvage divers based at the Norfolk Navy Base. They could certainly do this dive. We had worked with the Navy Salvage Command for many years, especially on the USS *Monitor* project, and had a great relationship. But now our target was just an unidentified bump on the sea floor, not the USS *Monitor*. In addition, Navy protocol would require one of their large salvage vessels to support the dive. Even if the Navy wanted to dive the site, getting time on those vessels wasn't possible until the following year. NOAA dive regulations also required a review process and special permission to dive to those depths, especially 30 miles offshore. But all we needed was a quick look at the bump and some still photos. Diving, if it could be done, was the quickest way to resolve the target and to move on, one way or another.

Despite these obstacles, we found a way to "unofficially" attempt to get divers onto the target before the season ended. I don't recall if we ever publicized this operation — probably not. Mike Overfield, who was my confederate, rented an appropriate dive boat and enlisted a few eager Navy divers to take a "recreational" dive offshore. It was a long ride out to the bump, about as far from shore as the dive boats go. But, before they got very far, the Hatteras weather closed in, and they had to abort. It wasn't worth contributing another boat to the so-called Graveyard of the Atlantic. The bump wasn't going anywhere so Mike and others started planning for next season.

New Plans for 2005

The critical focus of a new plan was to bring the right technology to identify the debris, if any, at the bump. The fathometer on the YP-679 had identified the bump as we passed over it in the "small position" box, created from the treasure salvors' Loran bearings. Given the times and position accuracy, the salvors' video could easily have been collected somewhere in the vicinity of the position they gave us. This time we wanted to thoroughly survey an area larger than just the position box with the bump in it. The most efficient and accurate way to do this was with an autonomous underwater vehicle (AUV). The AUV eliminated the need for towing, altitude control, carefully navigating the ship, and speed control. It would be programmed to drive along predetermined survey lines, maintaining the correct altitude until it completed its route. The sea state and surface weather didn't matter.

The NAVSEA autonomous underwater vehicle (AUV) in its transport case.

By 2005, AUVs had been around for a while, and NOAA had one or two that the Office of Coast Survey was beginning to use. We had the experience to use an AUV for the expedition and the Navy came through once again. The Naval Sea Systems Command (NAVSEA) provided an AUV along with its operators. The sonar imagery collected by the AUV would be downloaded from the recovered vehicle when the boat got back to port[15]. Given the previous year's problems, the NAVSEA AUV was our key survey tool.

RADM Cohen made the YP-679 available, and we planned the fall 2005 expedition around it. Since the events at Ocracoke the previous year were met with such enthusiasm and interest, we saw no need to repeat them in 2005, especially later in the year and deeper into the hurricane season, when the YP-679 was available. For all the advantages of using the YP-679, a big

---

15 This is unlike a towed unit with an optical cable that allows the imagery to be viewed in real time as it moves over the bottom.

The YP-679's "high" freeboard, with participants on board the vessel.

NAVSEA personnel practice an AUV launch from the sportfishing boat *Restless*.

disadvantage arose after NAVSEA made the AUV available for the expedition. As it turned out, we could neither launch nor recover the AUV from the YP-679 without specialized equipment. The vessel's freeboard was too high off the water to slip the AUV gently into the water and get it out.

Always resourceful, Mike Overfield rented the *Restless*, a 60-foot sport-fishing boat with a low freeboard to serve as the AUV launch-and-recovery platform. I suspect the *Restless* was the boat used in the aborted attempt to dive the bump at the end of the 2004 season. We would use the YP-679 primarily as the platform for towing the magnetometer and deploying a new ROV, BENTHOS, on any other target of interest. The BENTHOS ROV was more capable than the NOVA RAY, which was onboard the YP-679 the previous year. Equally important, the YP-679 could now bring aboard educators, museum professionals, and students to help develop STEM education programming. The goal was to develop lesson plans around the science, technology, and history of the search for the U.S. Navy's first submarine — hopefully, a compelling topic for students. These individuals could now be actual participants in the search and acquire that all-important "hands-on feel" for the science.

Operations Begin

In spring 2005, the hydrographic vessel NOAA Ship *Thomas Jefferson* made a transit in the vicinity of the larger *Alligator* search area. The *Thomas Jefferson* also made a similar cruise in June 2003, when we were forming our initial ideas of where to search. Both cruises were "cruises of opportunity," made possible by then-Captain Sam Debow of the NOAA Corps and head of NOAA's Office of Coast Survey. Over the previous two decades, Sam and I worked together many times and always

The Afloat Lab, a scientific and training vessel operated by the U.S. Office of Naval Research, will depart from North Carolina within the next few days in another attempt to find the USS Alligator.

Science turns fun in hunt for Civil War submarine

The YP-679 at Ocracoke garnered headlines from as far away as Philadelphia in 2005.

seemed to find a way to pool our resources on various projects. The *Thomas Jefferson* worked for Sam, who later became a RADM and commanded the entire NOAA Corps and all of NOAA's ship and aviation assets. The *Thomas Jefferson*'s side-scan sonar survey identified a number of addition uncommon bottom features in the area, warranting further investigation.

Ocracoke once again served as the "Home Port" for the YP-679. It was still the best place from which to access the search area off of Cape Hatteras. Additionally, the YP-679 and the *Restless* could be berthed side-by-side at Silver Lake Harbor. But in the weeks leading-up to the expedition's arrival at Ocracoke, concerns arose about unsettling weather. We were deeper into the hurricane season than in 2004, and 2005 was shaping up as a very active season. Hurricane Katrina had devastated the Gulf of Mexico just the month before. Keeping an alert eye to the weather, we proceeded with the expedition as planned. The return of the YP-679 to Ocracoke generated headlines as far away as Philadelphia.

Early morning on the day the expedition was to go to sea, a weather briefing was held to assess the offshore conditions. Offshore wave height was predicted to be between 4 and 6 feet, the absolute maximum at which the AUV could be launched and recovered safely. This day might be the only window before approaching weather would close in. So the *Restless*, with the AUV and the NAVSEA team aboard, left Ocracoke as soon as possible. The YP-679 followed later.

When the YP-679 departed Ocracoke and Hatteras Inlet, only a few who had sailed through the inlet the previous year were on board with Mike Overfield. As planned, almost a dozen educators, students, and communicators were on board to learn about the science and technology involved in the hunt for the *Alligator*. Including this new complement of people turned out to be fortuitous. Hurricane Ophelia arrived the next day and shut down offshore operations. The YP-679 could, however, remain in the sheltered waters of Silver Lake Harbor. This gave Mike a captive audience, and he thoroughly explained and demonstrated the "science" of exploration. Mike proved to be an inspiring teacher on that cruise. Later in the afternoon, a mandatory evacuation notice was issued for Ocracoke Island, and all the plans for the 2005 hunt for the *Alligator* came to an end.

Mike Overfield explains the science of ocean exploration on the YP-679's back deck.

Fortunately, the prior day's decision to take the *Restless* to sea and attempt to launch the AUV was wise. I have been on similar vessels in heavy seas when operations were questionable, and I know they can only be done safely with experienced personnel, especially a savvy captain. The captain must know his vessel well and understand its behaviors under various conditions; he has to have "the feel." The captain can position the vessel in exactly the right place in the waves, if only for 30 seconds, to get on or off a target, or to launch and recover. The captain of the *Restless* was such a person. The NAVSEA team was also expert at what they did. Thus, the AUV was deployed, swam its precise search pattern, and recovered.

The successful AUV deployment saved the day. We obtained detailed and accurate side-scan sonar images of the targeted bump as well as a wide area around it. We met the expedition's primary objective. The images were downloaded

The NAVSEA AUV on the surface about to begin its mission.

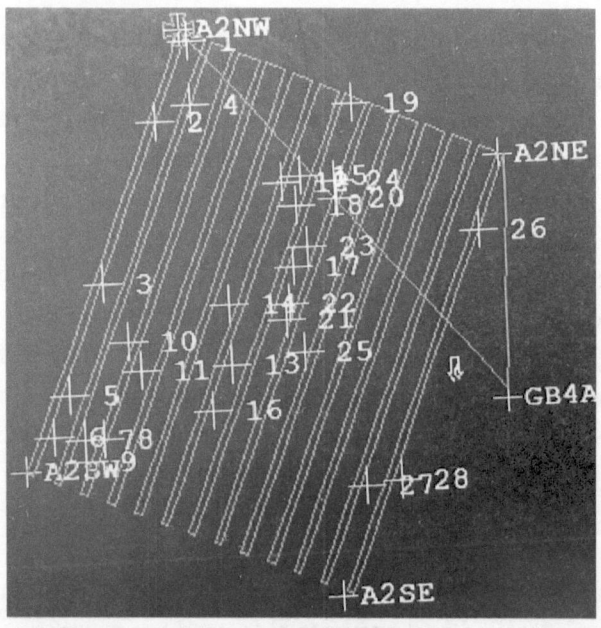

AUV side-scan sonar survey lines and the 28 individual contacts identified.

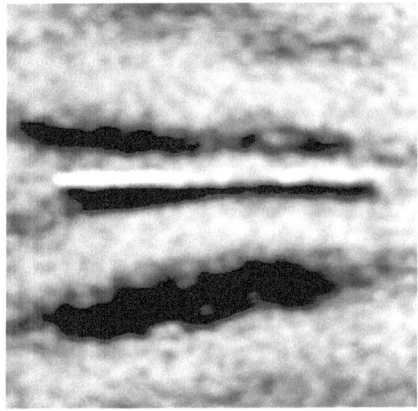

A side-scan sonar image of a "pipe" shape.

A side-scan sonar image of a straight-line feature believed to be a manmade object.

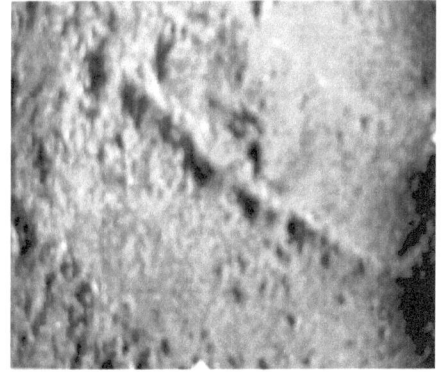

Below: Side-scan sonar images showing a prominent feature of interest, *left*, and a cylinder shape, *right*.

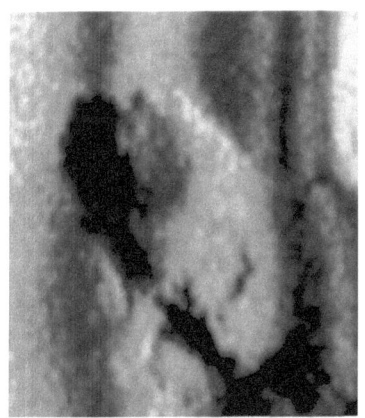
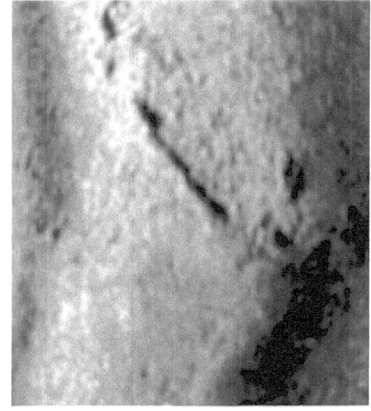

and taken to our offices in Silver Spring, Maryland, for a detailed examination and assessment.

Getting these images was pretty much the point where we had wanted to be in 2004, when so many things went wrong. Again, the Hatteras weather forced us ashore, but this time we had gathered the data we needed, or so we thought. At the end of the 2005 expedition, the question still remained: "Was there enough information in the images to determine that the debris at the bump was the remains of the USS *Alligator*?"

More Analysis

Upon returning to Silver Spring, we transferred the sonar images to one of our more powerful computers loaded with state-of-the-art image-processing software. The AUV had run 13 parallel and overlapping side-scan sonar survey lines within a small rectangle, approximately 500 meters on each side. The rectangle and survey lines straddled the target bump. In this small area, 28 individual contacts were identified on the bottom. Could these contacts be the remains of the *Alligator*? It felt a little like déjà vu. Two years before, we asked the same questions about a grainy 1986 videotape of the site: the one the salvors gave us.

But this time we had digital files and computer tools to help answer the question. We created separate image files for each contact, and then began the tedious task of analyzing each one. First, we applied digital filters and enlargement and enhancing techniques to each image. Then Mike Overfield, Bruce Terrell, and others pored over the images, straining their eyes and imaginations to identify objects that could be the remains of the *Alligator*. This process is more difficult than it may seem and requires many sets of eyes. It is easy to be fooled. I have seen this happen many times in my career. Imaging with side-scan sonar is like directing a flashlight over an object in a dark room, where the object's shadow reveals its shape. Everything that appears in a digital image can be accurately measured. Therefore, given the dimensions of the *Alligator*, only objects of a certain size could possibly be debris from the submarine.

There are ever-present problems with objects that have been on the bottom for nearly 150 years, especially small objects that can be "smothered" and hard to identify, even in a good photograph, never mind a sonar image. The natural processes of sedimentation, biologic action, and decomposition can disguise almost anything. If the *Alligator* had imploded and broken apart before reaching the bottom, positive identification would depend on unambiguously identifying an object or piece that can be proven to be part of the *Alligator*. Sometimes the only way to do this is to bring an object to the surface for analysis, even to a laboratory. But archeologists are loath to remove any object from its place until a site is fully understood. The physical relationship of one object to another is often important to the overall interpretation. Of course, as a shipwreck diver in those days, I would have brought any promising object to the surface to resolve the riddle — sooner rather than later.

After many hours and days of eye strain, we had analyzed all 28 images of the sonar contacts. For 20 of the images, we arrived at an "educated consensus guess" regarding what the object or shape might represent. The images we "guessed" at included: pipes, cylinders, prong-shaped depressions, straight-line shapes (indicating something man-made beneath the surface), vertical objects protruding above the surface, and prominent sizable objects of interest. The remaining 8 images had more subtle shapes that required further investigation to determine if they might be something of interest. Each object and shape was carefully measured, and, given their sizes, we concluded that all were within the dimensions of possible debris that could have come from the *Alligator*. But were they the remains of the *Alligator*?

This question continued to bedevil everyone. There simply was not enough information in the images to conclude that the debris was from the *Alligator*, nor was there enough to say it was definitely not. The conundrum continued. What now? Given the high degree of uncertainty and the enormous area in which the *Alligator* may have come to rest, did it make sense to leave the only potential site known and move on to look elsewhere? Everyone knew it would take multiple ships and years to search the area on the shelf where the *Alligator* could have landed. Plus, we would still be looking for an easy-to-miss needle in a very large haystack.

Four years after first hearing about the mysterious USS *Alligator*, and after two years of expeditions, a film production, and two symposiums, we were back to square one. We had, through circumstances, almost inadvertently drifted into the attempt to find it. Could we now leave the bump on the bottom unresolved and move on?

Third Symposium

An important feature from the beginning of the search was to build the largest community of interest possible. The *First Alligator Symposium*, which was held in October 2003 in Groton, Connecticut, at the Historic Ship USS *Nautilus* and Submarine Force Museum, followed the discovery of de Villeroi's original plans in Paris. It was the so-called "coming out party" that launched the *Alligator* into the minds of a broad spectrum of historians, archeologists, and inspired enthusiasts. It set the tone for the Discovery Science Channel film and drove both the expedition and filmmaking the following summer in August 2004.

On the heels of the highly publicized first expedition, a *Second Alligator Symposium* was held in October 2004 at the Nauticus, a maritime discovery center, in Norfolk, Virginia. This symposium aimed to update the community on new information about the *Alligator*, share our plans for a new expedition to build on the results of the summer's expedition, and to reveal the film that Dave Clark was making for the Discovery Science Channel. There was certainly a lot to report on. I think it fair to say that interest and enthusiasm increased, especially regarding the possibility that we might find the *Alligator*. Attendees at this symposium also began to appreciate the potential educational opportunities for Virginia schools. The symposiums proved to be a good idea on a number of levels. After the outcome of the 2005 expedition, we contemplated how a third symposium could further the hunt for the *Alligator*. Since the AUV images had been inconclusive, and the pressure to find the *Alligator* was still on.

The *Third Alligator Symposium* took place in November 2005 at the Independence Seaport Museum in Philadelphia. Unlike the previous symposiums, this one was billed as a series of workshops. Specifically, the workshops would: 1) summarize the historic research to date on the *Alligator*, its loss, and its inventor; 2) assess the outreach tools developed and refine ideas to create STEM educational programing; and 3) most importantly, discuss how to proceed in the search to find the *Alligator*. The most significant takeaway from the symposium was that the debris identified during the AUV survey had to be resolved before any new surveys should be undertaken. No one had a better idea of where to search, anyway. We would do our best in 2006, working with what would likely be diminishing resources.

But one thing was abundantly clear: We had to resolve the bump target driving us for the past two years — no matter what. As the year turned, we realized this was going to be more difficult than we envisioned. RADM Cohen retired from the U.S. Navy in January after an extraordinary naval career. The RADM, now civilian Jay Cohen, and I were the originators of rediscovering the USS *Alligator* and had jointly nurtured everything that followed. It was clear, at least to me, that the Navy would soon begin to lose interest in finding the *Alligator*. They would be happy for someone else to continue on, but it simply wasn't their job to locate it. Complicating matters further, the YP-679 was being retired and would no longer be available.

Mike Overfield, John Broadwater, and Dave Alberg put their creative minds together and proposed an extraordinary solution — acquire time on the U.S. Navy's NR1. The NR1 was a small nuclear research submarine, the only one in the world. It mounted perhaps the most sophisticated, underwater, remote-sensing technology then available, much of it classified. We had used the NR1 before in the Gulf of Mexico to investigate "special" areas and also along the East Coast to develop detailed images of the USS *Monitor*. The key to getting time on the NR1 was to petition during its training schedule or, if possible, when it was operating near the *Alligator* target site. The NR1's USS *Monitor* images made news around the world. It was good publicity for the Navy.

Navy's NR1

John Broadwater was the superintendent of the USS *Monitor* National Marine Sanctuary in 2004, when Jeff Johnson, who worked for him, put in a proposal to utilize time on the NR1. John was part of the 2004 expedition and had worked closely

The U.S. Navy's NR1 research submarine.

with Mike Overfield. The NR1 proposal was accepted and still active as the 2006 field season approached and became the basis for using the NR1 in the search for the USS *Alligator*. It didn't take long for everyone to grasp that the NR1 was the perfect solution to finally resolve the debris at the bump, as well as other possible debris targets in our search vicinity. All the sensing equipment, technicians, and crew would be on board the NR1. It was the perfect solution!

We decided that Mike Overfield and Dave Alberg would go aboard the NR1 and, working with the executive officer and crew, ride the submarine to the search area and conduct the survey. Dave Alberg, who was the former vice president of the Nauticus maritime discovery center, helped create the *Second Alligator Symposium*, which took place at the center in 2004. Before going aboard the NR1, Dave joined NOAA to take over the Monitor

The NR1 and its mothership, the *Carolyn Chouest*, off of Cape Henry, Virginia.

National Marine Sanctuary when John Broadwater moved on to other responsibilities in the Maritime Heritage Program.

There was no fanfare in 2006, in contrast to 2004 and 2005. In fact, the public was generally unaware of the new survey. Anyone at sea in the vicinity would witness nothing. The NR1 would travel to the site and conduct the survey while submerged, just as German U-boats had prowled this same area during World War II. Depending on circumstances, the NR1 would also search for the *William Rockefeller*, a 14,000-ton tanker sunk nearby by a German U-boat in June 1942. At the time of its sinking, the *William Rockefeller* was one of the largest tankers in the world and is, today, the largest tanker lost off the North Carolina coast in the Graveyard of the Atlantic.

But our primary task was to resolve the AUV side-scan sonar targets identified the year before. One way or another, we would determine if the debris targets were the remains of the USS *Alligator*. Finally, after nearly three frustrating years, we were about to have our answer. I remember musing about how fitting it was that we would be searching for the U.S. Navy's first submarine, a modern marvel for its time, with the Navy's first and only nuclear research submarine, a modern marvel for its time. It was symbolic of the tremendous development in submarines in scarcely a hundred years.

Mike and Dave went aboard a chartered Navy vessel and made the 32-mile journey offshore to rendezvous with the NR1 and its mothership, the *Carolyn Chouest*, off of Cape Henry, Virginia. There was no fanfare or press.

The NR1, launched in 1969 and 147 feet in length, carried a crew of three officers, eight enlisted personnel, and two scientists. It had an operating depth of 3,000 feet. NR1 was built primarily to conduct missions such as search and recovery, geological surveys, and oceanographic research. When it was launched, it was one of the deepest diving submarines in the world. It had the unique capability to remain at a site and completely map or search an area with a high degree of accuracy. But the NR1 was a relatively slow craft, traveling at about 4.5 knots on the surface and 3.5 knots when submerged, which is still the case with deep-diving research submarines. Also, like all deep-diving research submarines, the NR1 had view ports built into the hull and external video cameras, which allowed for direct visual observation. The *Carolyn Chouest*'s primary job was to tow the NR1 to its operating area and then tow it back to port after the operation was completed. Mike and Dave would take the two scientists' berths when they went aboard the NR1.

On November 7, Mike and Dave arrived at the rendezvous and went directly aboard the NR1. The *Carolyn Chouest* began the tow south in heavy 20-foot seas. They stayed on board the NR1 until November 11, when the survey was completed. The challenging seas more than doubled the time planned to get to the search area, and the NR1 was in tow for over 28 hours. She remained submerged while being towed at about 150 feet beneath the surface to avoid being battered. Both the USS *Monitor* and USS *Alligator* were towed in these very waters in heavy seas and were lost. The formidable *Carolyn Chouest* simply plowed ahead, and the NR1 and those aboard rode in relative comfort beneath the surface and turbulence. Times have changed since 1862 and 1863.

It's Just Debris

The NR1 traversed a survey pattern, blanketing the search area and locating all of the sonar contacts identified and analyzed in 2005. The rolling sea above made no difference as the NR1 cruised about 60 feet off the bottom. Every 2005 contact and others in the vicinity were thoroughly investigated, including an "eyes on" visual inspection.

Finally, we had an answer to the riddle of the debris, the bump, and the grainy images from the 1986 drop-camera video. All proved to be mostly geological or forms of modern debris. Only a spooled cable draped across a rock outcropping stood out. Nothing at the bump or in the vicinity had anything to do with the USS *Alligator*. Finally, the hard facts were now clear. The *Alligator* was still missing and waiting to be found.

After returning to Silver Spring, Mike and Dave didn't articulate any great disappointment. The NR1 ride had been a wonderful experience for them both. Neither had ever been on

A last look: Jim Christley's artistic depiction of the search for the Alligator.

a research submarine, and the NR1 was certainly the Cadillac of these submarines. There must have been a feeling of both relief to finally have resolved the bump and, at the same time, a little sorrow to have not made one of the great marine archeological finds of the century. But that is the nature of archeology — the search is never over!

When the NR1 returned to the *Carolyn Chouest*, Mike and Dave transferred to the vessel in a "rib," or rigid inflatable boat, to make the nearly four-day cruise back to Groton, Connecticut, home port of the NR1. Its missions for 2006 had come to an end. Shortly after this mission, the NR1 was decommissioned and followed the *Alligator* into the annals of U.S. naval history as one of the most advanced submarines of its time. Mike and Dave were among the last scientists to ride on the NR1.

Despite the outcomes, Mike Overfield and Dave Alberg were not deterred, and they were already thinking about the next phase of the search for the elusive *Alligator*. At this point, no one even knew they had been at sea continuing the search, except for the fact that Dave had slipped, broken his arm, and lost his laptop while transferring from the rib to the *Carolyn Chouest*. He had to explain how he had broken his arm and account for the missing laptop. The waters off of Cape Hatteras were not kind to any of the *Alligator* expeditions. The Graveyard of the Atlantic only begrudgingly gives up its secrets.

The grainy 1986 videotape, which dropped on the scene at seemingly the exact right time in 2004, combined with the calamity on board the YP-679, had created the proverbial perfect storm. It drove everything up to and including the NR1 cruise. But what was actually on that grainy tape? After the NR1 survey, it now seemed clear. The salvors may have interpreted the spooled cabling over the rock outcropping as a propeller, and the port hole they identified was probably a dark spot of biologic growth on the outcropping. The other debris just confused matters further. Such are the tricks the ocean plays on those who search for things in it, especially when combined with the burning desire to see what one is looking for.

While we didn't find the Alligator, the expeditions, symposiums, and spin-offs, spurred by the grainy video, brought benefits to many, long outlasting the search. But, after 2006, this phase of the hunt for the USS *Alligator* had come to an end.

Chapter 10
Aftermath and Spinoffs

At the conclusion of the active search for the USS *Alligator* in 2006, everyone involved thought that the *Alligator* might never be found. The salvors' bump drove our earlier hope, but now it was clear that continuing the search could take years — many years — and perhaps only divine providence could lead us to the remains of the now-famous submarine. For those inspired by the *Alligator* story, this reality was difficult to accept. But, even at this point, we hadn't entirely given up, and we continued to scheme about how to keep the search alive.

Survey-of-Opportunity Program

We realized we would never again possess the resources to continue the search over such a vast area, so we thought about involving others. The idea was that university, government, and privately owned research ships transiting the search area could participate by surveying "track lines of opportunity" as they navigated from point to point. Mike Overfield constructed a survey grid of the entire area. Using this grid, a vessel's navigators could select any convenient, un-surveyed track line, navigate the track line with their gear, and transmit the imagery for analysis. If this worked, large sections of the search area would be surveyed, and, if providence lent a hand, we might stumble on the *Alligator*. I have seen a good hunch or a stroke of luck pan out now and again, but counting on it is never a good idea. The idiom "like looking for a needle in a haystack" is used for good reason — the needles are never found.

The survey-of-opportunity idea was a longshot. Nonetheless, we designed a prototype website as the basis for the program. For a short time, participation looked promising. But, after 2007, interest in the *Alligator* and its story began to wane and so did the interest in a survey-of-opportunity program. Without a new discovery or compelling news items — such as Catherine's discovery in Paris — the interest simply ran out. In the end, I am afraid we disappointed a lot of *Alligator* enthusiasts. Even so, we continued to receive calls and emails for many years thereafter, always asking, "When are you going back to find the *Alligator*?" The saga of the mysterious *Alligator* continues to this day, if only at a low boil.

Was It Worth It?

One way to answer the question of whether the effort to rediscover the USS *Alligator* was worth it — when, in the end, we never found it, brought it home, or paraded it around — is to consider the effects of the journey and continuing interest. In 2007, the Discovery Science Channel's official DVD release of Dave Clark's film, *Hunt for the U.S.S. Alligator: U.S. Navy's First Sub*, spurred an uptick in interest in the mysterious, lost submarine. But I think much of the continuing interest is driven by the fact that the *Alligator* is still out there, and the final story has yet to be told. The mystery and the challenge remain.

Perhaps there was a slight silver lining to the clouds that literally hung over us for the three frustrating years we spent looking for the *Alligator*. So much was learned by so many during the journey. The impacts of the spinoffs and related activities may far outweigh the value of actually finding the *Alligator* itself — at least for now. I know that when we began the journey, I hadn't perceived the spinoffs that would emerge. But good people just naturally found value in every step we made along the way. To enumerate them all is a story for another time, but those that stand out in my mind are as follows.

STEM Education Spinoff

Educators in the National Marine Sanctuary system were the first to grasp that the application of the science of remote sensing and technology in the search for the *Alligator* provided a basis for teaching STEM education in classrooms. They concluded that — together with the knowledge of meteorology, oceanography, and physics needed to even hazard a guess as to where to search — the hunt for the *Alligator* might provide a well-rounded and engaging curriculum. The underlying idea was that students who were not interested in science might want to help solve a mystery: a Civil War mystery to determine the *Alligator*'s location. This required that they learn some history and how to research history. Educational spinoffs could demonstrate ways to capture the imagination of many of our nation's youth, helping move ocean science and exploration forward — and inspiring future scientists and historians along the way. I think the educators did that to some extent.

The educators developed "Hunt for the Alligator" lesson plans on bathymetry, sedimentation, weather, air and water pressure, history, material corrosion science and conservation, the technology of exploration, and tides and currents. All of these topics were presented within the context of helping to find the *Alligator*. The lesson plans and more were made available online. Educators from many institutions participated in the development and use of the lesson plans. These institutions included the Philadelphia Seaport Museum, Graveyard of the Atlantic Museum, Stone Ridge School of the Sacred Heart, PAST Foundation, Institute for Exploration, Nauticus Maritime Museum, National Underwater Research Center at the University of Connecticut, and a number of NOAA offices. The educational programs of every National Marine Sanctuary around the country shared the lesson plans with all of their local partner schools. Many young students were exposed to science through the "Hunt for the *Alligator*."

Perhaps the best example of STEM education through the Hunt for the *Alligator* took place in local schools in Norfolk, Virginia, where a full-semester course was developed and offered to students as an elective. More than 100 students eventually took the course. But, as in such matters, it's impossible to know the full extent to which the Hunt for the *Alligator* propelled STEM education. For a time, however, it was front and center in creative ways to attract young minds to science.

Museums Keep the Story Alive

It is safe to say that the story of the *Alligator* became known in maritime history museums around the world as well as in other museums that focused on technology or history in general. The discovery of de Villeroi's original plans in Paris generated the type of headlines that rarely occur in the museum world. Many museums contacted us — Team *Alligator* — to learn more so they could develop exhibits telling the *Alligator* story. Museum representatives attended each of the three symposiums and some even partook in the events at Ocracoke and aboard the YP-679. We made every effort to take advantage of their interests, providing them with background information, such as text, pictures, and images. In some cases, we even helped them to create exhibits. Most museums also purchased Dave Clark's film, and I know of a few that hosted public viewings. Lastly, we produced simple, portable exhibit materials, which we sent out to museums.

Over time, museums replaced many *Alligator* exhibits (originally temporary exhibits by design) with other, more timely ones. However, in a number of museums that are more closely associated with the Graveyard of the Atlantic and submarines, the *Alligator* exhibits remain. These museums include the Mariners Museum in Newport News, Virginia; Graveyard of the Atlantic Museum in Hatteras, North Carolina; Nauticus Maritime Museum in Norfolk, Virginia; and Historic Ship USS *Nautilus* and Submarine Force Museum in Groton, Connecticut. Museums help ensure the *Alligator* will not be "lost" again and will maintain a place in history.

Maritime Heritage Moved Forward

Perhaps the biggest beneficiary of the *Alligator* search was the fledgling Maritime Heritage Program we were creating in the Office of National Marine Sanctuaries within NOAA. In the four years between 2002 and 2006, the program transformed from a few historians and archeologists working somewhere in the Sanctuary system, to a recognizable program. The previously unknown mystery of the *Alligator* created national attention and brought a cadre of new partnerships. These spanned the spectrum, from universities, museums, corporations, and history associations, to government agencies and even foreign governments. Tim Runyon and John Broadwater were important leaders during this transitional time.

These key years set the foundation for the evolving Maritime Heritage Program over the next decade. The program eventually included the discovery of other iconic lost ships and helped to make maritime heritage an important consideration in marine protected area planning and management. Perhaps the most important outcome of the continuing search for lost ships of significance was the emergence of the broader concept of maritime culture landscapes. Just as the *Alligator* has meaning only in the context of the American Civil War and the development of submarine technology, all lost ships have meaning only in the context of the maritime landscapes of their time. The effort to rediscover the USS *Alligator* inadvertently became an important part of rediscovering maritime cultural landscapes.

Interest Continues

The hunt for the *Alligator* prompted many individuals to undertake their own related efforts. These manifested in new books and websites as well as research and search efforts by enthusiasts. One such example was a renewed search for de Villeroi's Propeller, the Infernal Machine that Philadelphia newspapers once reported to be in the Delaware River. The Propeller is considered the *Alligator*'s prototype and is sometimes referred to as "*Alligator* Júnior."[16]

In fact, it was after the U.S. Navy viewed the Propeller that they entered into the contract with de Villeroi to build the submarine that became the USS *Alligator*. The fate of the

---

16 See: 1861 article shown page 26.

Propeller isn't clear. The rumor or legend is that it was used or dumped in a channel construction project. Most believe it lies buried beneath the mud and covered in dense vegetation in what is now nearby marshland. Enthusiasts in Philadelphia have reasoned that the Propeller would be much easier to find in the marshes than the *Alligator*, which was lost at sea. I must admit that there may be merit to their claims. But the Propeller was not the U.S. Navy's first submarine. Neither the Navy nor NOAA, therefore, had much interest in pursuing its whereabouts. We did, however, make a trip to the marsh with a group of enthusiasts. It was clear that finding the Propeller somewhere deep in the mud would be no easy feat. At this writing, the Propeller remains to be discovered. Maybe someday, a crane operator excavating foundations for a new development project will rediscover history.

Sometimes people still ask me why we could not find the *Alligator* and when it will be found. I guess I can now say: "Read the book!"

Epilogue

All things move in cycles, and the interest in the still-undiscovered USS *Alligator* is no different. But where is the *Alligator* in its cycle? The mystery was solved, and the story of the *Alligator* and its inventor, Brutus de Villeroi, was revealed in Dave Clark's film. Much later, any remaining curiosity in de Villeroi was more than satisfied in Chuck Veit's 2018 book. All told, the interest cycle for the *Alligator* has settled into a steady state. Now it's just another 19th century submarine that has not been found. Much information is available on the internet, but little or no new details have been added. Some websites are no longer maintained and hard to access. Most importantly, a "new search of discovery" has not been contemplated or undertaken since our 2006 NR1 expedition. Considering the long view, however, this is the natural cycle of how interest in discovery first peaks, then diminishes, waiting to be rekindled. Then new enthusiasts discover the story — and the search begins again.

An encouraging factor is that the capabilities of autonomous underwater vehicles and their sensors have evolved in leaps and bounds since the 2006 NR1 expedition. Interest in finding the *Alligator* may again swing upward, if only to demonstrate new technological capabilities on a newsworthy target of historic value. Indeed, the technology may now be available to search large areas of seafloor with a far better chance of finding the *Alligator*.

Mike Overfield presented ideas on how to limit the search. In fact, he was still ruminating on defining a more practical search area when he passed away unexpectedly in 2009. He never lost his fascination with and interest in finding the *Alligator*. With Mike Overfield's passing, the Hunt for the *Alligator* lost its most charismatic champion. I think he might have found a way to go out searching again. Mike Overfield serves as a beacon for those who would take up the search. As pointed out to me by Tony Reyer, Mike's close companion on the 2004 expedition, Mike shared a number of Brutus de Villeroi's finest traits: the energy and fascination to always imagine what others could not.

By 2010, the evolving Maritime Heritage Program was nearing its apogee, thanks, in no small measure, to the Hunt for the *Alligator*, and the efforts of Tim Runyon, James Delgado, and others. The program was arguably a leader in maritime heritage and discovery, continuing as such for almost a decade. Many of the program's individuals and their colleagues were participants in the Hunt for the *Alligator*.

The official Team *Alligator* patch.

RADM Cohen (Jay) and I have remained close friends since that day in 2002 in the South Pacific and, after our retirements, are even more so. Steve Burns and I continue to meet periodically and discuss ideas, and he still helps me out in some of the things I get involved in — *pro bono*, of course. He continues to use his skills and influence to support good causes through film. Dave Clark and I literally run into each other in Rock Creek Park, Washington, D.C., where we both jog. We can't help but hang out for a while and reminisce. Jim Christley lives in Arizona and continues to pursue his art, and, together, we share sea stories. Bruce Terrell retired and moved back to his beloved Richmond, Virginia, where he is no doubt working on Civil War projects. After almost ten years of managing the Monitor National Marine Sanctuary and championing the discovery and interpretation of shipwrecks in the Graveyard of the Atlantic, Dave Alberg joined the National Park Service and is stationed in Alaska. The arm he broke on the NR1 expedition never fully healed. John Broadwater, after publishing his seminal work on the USS *Monitor* and retiring from federal service, remains an active marine archeologist, working on Civil War projects. Catherine Marzin is still at NOAA and continues to visit her family in France. Michiko Martin moved on to the U.S. Forest Service, blazing a path from Naval officer to chief forester in the Southwest. Dwight Coleman became the director of the Inner Space Center at the University of Rhode Island and is heavily involved in exploration. And what about Bob Ballard? Well, we have done quite a number of things together since that day in the South Pacific in 2002 when the Hunt for the *Alligator* began. He simply remains Bob Ballard, the paragon of ocean exploration.

As for the United States Navy, Civil War historians now recognize the USS *Alligator* as the U.S. Navy's first submarine.

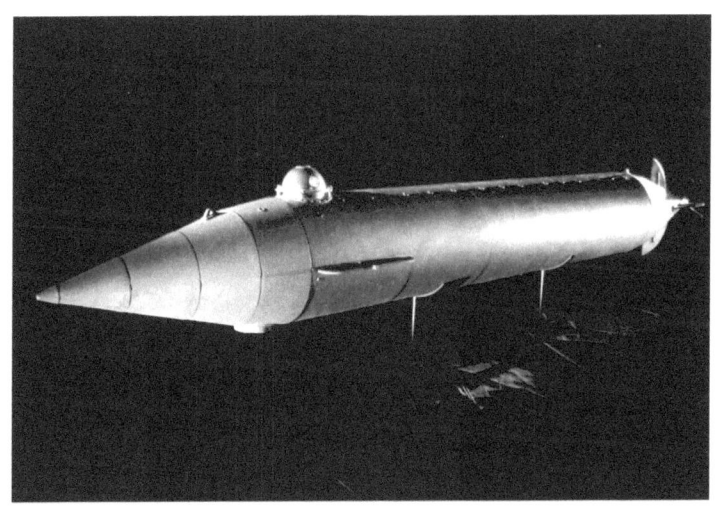

Photo of a scale model of the USS *Alligator* in the test tank at the U.S. Navy's test facility in Carderock, Maryland.

Appendix A

Alligator as Designed by de Villeroi for the U.S. Navy

These drawings were discovered by Catherine Marzin at the Service Historique de la Marine. They depict de Villeroi's original design, which was powered by oar propulsion, and have been annotated for clarity.

1. Inboard Profile

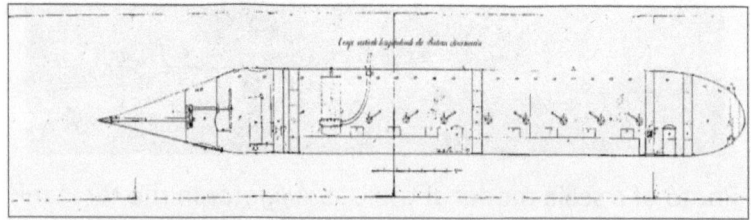

2. Inboard Deck Plan

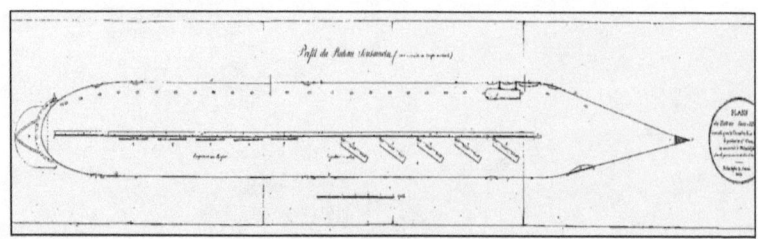

3. Main Deck Plan

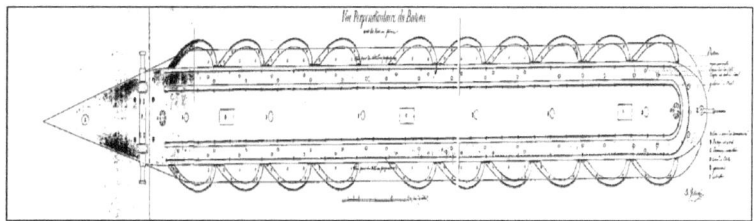

4. Outboard Profile

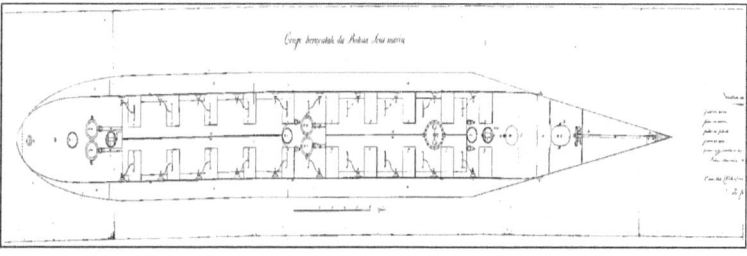

Appendix B

Submarine Propeller Designed by de Villeroi for the French Navy

These drawings were found at the Service Historique de la Marine along with de Villeroi's drawings of the *Alligator*. They are de Villeroi's drawings for the submarine he proposed to the French Navy. Their scale differs from the *Alligator* drawings.

1. Inboard Profile

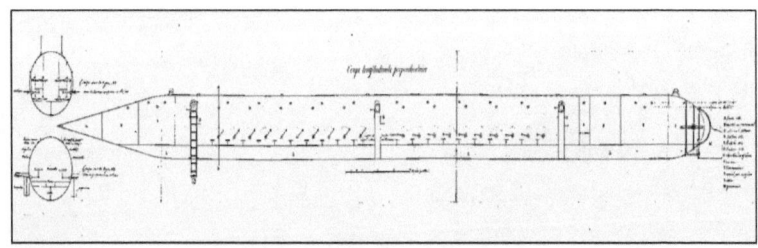

2. Inboard Deck Plan

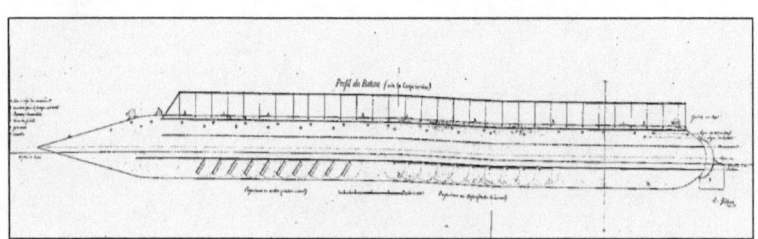

3. Main Deck Plan

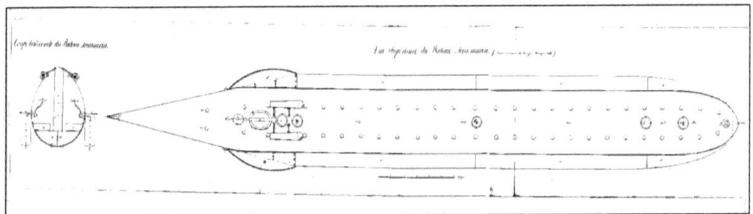

4. Outboard Profile

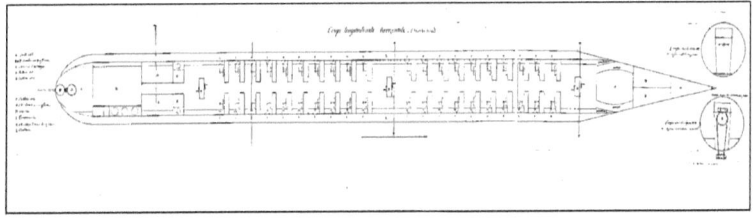

Appendix C

1861 Contract Agreement to Build the USS *Alligator*

This agreement, made and entered into this first day of November, A.D. one thousand eight hundred and sixty-one, between Martin Thomas of one part and the United States by Gideon Welles, Secretary of the Navy on the other part, witnessed:

First: The party of the first part will construct and deliver to the party of the second part within forty (40) days from the date of this agreement, an Iron Submarine Propeller of the plan of M. de Villeroi, at least fifty six inches (56") in width and sixty six (66") inches in height and forty five feet in length, for the sum of fourteen thousand dollars ($14,000) to be paid when completed and delivered, ready for use within ten days after delivery and certificate is in all respects ready for service.

Second: The government of the United States will employ M. de Villeroi to superintend the construction of said propeller, as well as in its employment for actual service when required, and agrees to pay him for his full services at the rate of two thousand dollars per annum whilst thus employed, his pay to commence with the date of this agreement: also to pay reasonable wages to the crew of said propeller, and to transport it from Philadelphia to the place or places where the Secretary of the Navy directs it to be used.

Third: In case the said de Villeroi shall perform valuable services with said propeller for the United States by the destruction of an enemy's ship or vessel by direction of the Secretary of the Navy and to his satisfaction, then the government of the United States shall pay to the party of the first part a further sum of eighty-six thousand dollars ($86,000) subject to and appropriated by Congress.

Fourth: The secret of said invention shall be divulged by the inventor, M. de Villeroi, under his solemn oath or affirmation in a written paper subscribed by him to be sealed and deposited with the Chief of Bureau of Yards and Docks, with the certificate thereon of Mr. W.L. Hirst that he has carefully examined the paper and firmly believes it to be of the secret of said invention, not to be opened until after the payment of said eighty six thousand dollars ($86,000), or the death, disability or dereliction of duty of the inventor shall occur. [Bolding added to emphasize the secrecy attributed to the invention.]

Fifth: The said invention shall not be used by or the secret divulged to any government, power or individual without the consent in writing of both parties to this agreement.

In the presence of S. Gough
/s/ Martin Thomas
/s/ Gideon Welles

Appendix D

Selected USS *Alligator* Correspondence

1. Excerpt from May 1, 1861, letter on the launch of *Alligator* from William L. Hirst to Commodore Joseph Smith (BuYards and Docks)

"The boat proved remarkably buoyant and requires four or six tons of lead for ballast: The Propelling fins were found to work with ease and the only fear Mr. Thomas entertained was on that point and it is now removed. [The six tons of ballast is reasonable with the immersion/inch calculations I did and can be sent.]."

2. Description of the *Alligator* from an article of the period

"She is 46 feet in length, about 6 feet deep and 4 feet 6 inches in breadth. In shape and appearance, she is much like a large iron boiler flattened with a tapering or conical end, and a rounded stern. A sheet iron guard runs around the outside of the vessel under which the hand paddles, 8 on a side, are attached. These are two leaved and the leaves close on the upward or back stroke to avoid the resistance of the water. Their handles, to which the paddles are at right angles, pass through the iron sides of the vessel, and are moved by the rower, the iron rod or handle acting as a hinge.

Inside she looks somewhat like a bomb-proof man of war barge with white painted iron thwarts at regular intervals, and an arched iron roof perforated with small, glazed apertures.

On her conical bow is a watertight compartment connected by a small door with the main interior space, and having in the bottom a little round door called a 'manhole' through which a diver in submarine armor may descent descend to the bottom of the water and carry on his destructive work at leisure and unobserved. There is a fan like rudder, of a crescent shape, hinged on the stern, fastened at its horns to the top and bottom of the end. The vessel contains pumps, and air condenser, anchor, etc., and is entered by a manhole on the top near the bow."

3. **May 31, 1862, report by Samuel Eakins on the "State of the *Alligator*"**

Sir,

By order of yourself as communicated to me by Wm. L. Hirst Esq I assumed charge of the Submarine Propeller lying at the Navy Yard Philadelphia and report to yourself for duty on the 14th ult. I have since been diligently engaged in the duty assigned me and I now report this date May 31, [1862].

1st The absence of all the air tubes and couplings necessary for communication with the air pumps and air chamber of the boat. As well as pipes and couplings belonging to the apparatus for distributing the air through the boat. All of which had evidently at one time been in place but could not now be found. These have since been replaced and the proper examinations made to ascertain the completeness of the other fittings. These examinations disclosed a number of leaks and de Villeroi was given three days to make the repairs at the Navy Yard. During this time, so many leaks were discovered from the Air Chamber around the flanges, bulkheads as to make the return of the boat to the yard of the builders a necessity. [This shows a lack of planning for testing systems and possibly for problems in assembly of components.]

2nd The want of a lookout place has been supplied. For this it was to take off the upper covering of the entrance to the boat and prepare patterns and castings and this the workmen are now fitting in place. The covering of the entrance to the diver's room has been altered and refitted and is now reliable and alteration has also been made on the door of exit for the divers that will improve it, and I hope may be extremely efficient and sure in its closing.

The arrangement for discharge of ballast was very defective. The lever handles being entirely too short as well as being hid away among the pipes for filling and discharging the water from the tank. New levers have been made for these and they are placed in such a position as to be immediately available and true in operations. [Again, a lack of testing and a design flaw.]

A water pressure gauge and level have been placed in position upon the boat and vent cocks inserted in the tanks which will insure their filling. The paddles have been overhauled and made sure of being in good working order. I have repainted the outside and a portion of the inside of the boat and some minor alterations made of the internal arrangement making the parts easier of access by the crew for working and adding to the efficiency of the boat.

Very Respectfully
Samuel Eakin.

[I will send a detailed response to the Selfridge report later on.]

4. **August 8, 1862, Report on the Readiness of the *Alligator* by Thos. O. Selfridge, Lieutenant, Commanding Submarine Boat *Alligator***

Sir: In obedience to your orders, I have the honor to make the following report upon the submarine boat Alligator, of which I am in charge, founded upon personal examination and experiments with her.

This submarine boat, as I understand, was to have possessed the following properties:

1st   Facilities of immersion and emersion.

2nd   Self propulsion above and below the water.

3rd   Capability of remaining with her crew a long time under water, by purifying the air contained in her, so as to admit of its being re-inhaled repeatedly, &c.

4th   To be able to operate under water, and to permit a person to pass in and out at pleasure.

Most of these properties she does not possess to a practical degree, and in all she is defective.

1st   Facilities of immersion and emersion. Her apparatus for sinking and rising is good, and sufficient for the purpose. She is incapable however of being suspended in the water, but must sink when once immersed to the bottom, therefore she could only operate in such depth of water, that a person standing upon her could reach the vessel above him.

2nd   Propulsion above and below the water. She is in this particular very defective, being totally incapable of stemming an ordinary tide of the velocity of 1½ knots, and she is from her low rate of speed and length, difficult to manage with any exactness with the helm. Her ventilation is bad, even above water with the manhole open. On one occasion after her crew had been in her an hour, two of them became so exhausted as to be lifted from inside, and the remainder were all so prostrated, as to be obligated to leave the inside and to get in boats that were near, or upon her outside. As to propulsion under water, she has never been tried, but in this respect, it is hardly probable she could do any better than on the surface.

3rd   Capability of remaining under water. She has no means known to me of purifying and replenishing the vitiated air other than *forcing it through lime water. This, though it would absorb much of the carbonic acid, would be only but partial relief. With her crew of twenty-two persons, it would not be safe to remain more than an hour under the surface.*

4th *To be able to operate under the water. I cannot see that this submarine boat in its present state could be of any use in this particular. The means proposed by the inventor may be very pretty in theory, but in practice, they would not in my opinion be at all applicable.*

By means of an air chamber, which is filled with compressed air, a person can get in and out of her but there are no means of supplying that person with air other than a common tube connecting with the mouth. It is extremely improbable that any person could be found who with only this slight means of obtaining air would remain any time under water. Such a person would be obligated to keep one hand on his nostrils and would have to be loaded as to remain below the surface, a position that would admit of little exertion upon his part.

To sum up the whole, I consider that this vessel has such inherent defects as to preclude of her use as her name indicates for submarine purposes. If her speed was greatly increased, her steering apparatus improved and she could receive a much better ventilation, she might be made use of to operate above the surface. The manner in which she could be brought in play in this particular is very limited, confined to approaching an enemy at night, and liable in this respect to be easily frustrated by a boat pulling near the vessel to be attacked.

It seems to me, therefore under all the circumstances, of doubtful expediency to proceed any further in improvements upon her. I have the honor to be, very respectfully, your obedient servant,

Thos. O. Selfridge, Lieutenant, Commanding Submarine Boat Alligator.

5. July 17, 1862, Letter Directing the Re-fit of the *Alligator* at the Washington Naval Yard

HON. Gideon Welles
Secretary of the Navy
Washington, D.C.

Bureau of Yards and Docks
17 July 1862

Sir

You will be pleased to have the stern of the Submarine Propeller at the yard extended and such alterations made as may be necessary to use a propeller instead of the 'fins' as per the plan enclosed.

Respectfully
Your Obedient Servant
Joseph Smith

Captain A. A. Harwood
Washington

Appendix E

Derived Technical Description of the USS *Alligator*

By James Christley

Length:
47 feet. This is variously given as anywhere from 45 to 50 feet. It is neither clear nor defined as to how the 47 feet was measured. When it was decided to remove the oars and install a screw propeller, the boat was authorized to be lengthened. How much is not known.

Beam:
56 inches as given by the specifications. This is the hull beam. The overall beam over the oar guards is given as over 80 inches.

Height:
Height of main hull is 66 inches. It is not known how much the observation dome added to this height, nor is it clear how high the air tube might have extended.

Hull Construction:
Rolled and hammered iron plate varying in thickness from ¼ to 3/8 inches (9 to 12 mm as a spec given in the notes to de Villeroi drawings). This thickness corresponds to 10-to-15-pound (per square foot) plate. The fastening method was riveting as arc welding was unknown at the time. It is not known

what riveting method was used (lap, but with lap plate, double lap, etc.). Viewing the existing illustrations, it seems to be that, but the plates were butted then backed by a thinner lap plate and through riveted with the outside head countersunk and planed smooth. The rivet pattern, rivet size and spacing were estimated by using the formulae in Marshall's "Elementary Machine Drawing and Design" of 1912. It is assumed that much of the formulations in this, and other mechanical engineering texts of the late 19th and early 20th centuries reflect accurately the practices of metal workers of the Civil War period. It is assumed that 3/8 inch plate was used thus giving the dimensions as follows:

Rivet Shaft Diameter: 7/8 inch
Rivet Head Diameter: 1½ inches
Rivet Pitch: 2½ inches

There may have been a system of internal stiffening by the use of inner circumferential ribs. If used, they would have been similar in thickness to the plates and from ½ to 1 inch wide in the web. They may have been rolled angles.

There were two internal bulkheads which defined the diver lockout chamber in the forward end of the boat. These would have been made of flat plate of the same thickness as the hull. It is likely they would have been riveted to circumferential angle frames. The aft most of the bulkhead would have had a large opening for an entrance hatch. The opening would have circumferentially stiffened with a doubling plate.

Hull Form:
The hull was originally designed with a conical section forward, a parallel midbody and a rounded stern. The sectional shape of the midbody was roughly egg shaped with the widest part of the beam at below the vertical centerline of the hull. See de Villeroi's drawings for details of the hull form.

Penetrations:
The following hull penetrations are known. Along the top of the hull near the top centerline are a line of 36 glass "bulls' eyes." These are installed to allow light to penetrate to the inside of the boat for illumination. The detail of how these were installed is not known. It is surmised that they were thick sections of glass sandwiched between bolted (screwed) flanges with flax or gutta-percha gasketing.

An observation dome replaced the access hatch forward. Eakin found there was no way to see out while underway unless the hatch was open. Being unsatisfactory in his mind, he had a dome cast. There are no drawings known of this dome so its shape and fastening method has been surmised.

There were nine pairs of oars approximately 30 inches apart with their horizontal shafts extending through the hull. These penetrations were most likely similar to the packing glands used on steam engines and valves. Generically called "stuffing tubes," they would have been bolted to the hull, with the major portion of the stuffing tube on the inside.

The propeller shaft penetration and the extension of the stern to accommodate the propeller and gearing are not known. It is assumed the shaft penetration would have been a scaled stuffing tube type penetration.

There were five internal tubes which were mounted on the centerline and spaced throughout the boat. Two were closed at the bottom and open at the top and housed the buoyancy chambers. Three were closed at the top and open at the bottom and housed the emergency release weights.

Rudder pintle hull penetrations were most likely specially cast stuffing tube type fittings bolted to the top and bottom of the hull plating. These would be similar in design but differently sized than the oar stuffing tubes.

Buoyancy Chambers:
No written description of the operation of these has been located. It was assumed given the scaled size from the drawings that the chambers would have provided about 130 pounds of positive buoyancy if released to the surface. It was found by David Merriman when he actually operated his model of the submarine in the test tank at the Navy's David Taylor Naval Testing Center's model basin that the chambers provided a great deal of depth control and longitudinal stability when deployed but not surfaced.

Emergency Release Weights:
Three tubes in the boat housed emergency release weights. This consisted of a stack of either iron cylinders or lead cylinders held in place by a rotating latch mechanism. Upon release, the weights would give additional positive buoyancy to the boat, and it was hoped to allow it to surface if in trouble.

There were an unknown number of piping hull penetrations for flooding the ballast tanks and for pumping water out of the tanks. The flanging of this connection is assumed to be a standard bolted flange connection with a leather or similar material gasketing. The size of the opening is scaled from the drawing. This size flange would require four or six bolts, square headed and from ½ to 1 inch in diameter.

There is an air tube penetration on the top of the hull. The flanging of this connection is similar to that used for the air tube cited above.

Propulsion:
The prototype for the Alligator had a single hand crank operated screw propeller. De Villeroi decided that for the Alligator,

he would abandon that method and use a set of hand operated oars of his own design. He made this decision to trade speed for maneuverability. The oars, he indicated in a letter, "The boat moves by the means of 18 side propellers, invisible above the water. It can turn round in a small space and will sail backward in case of necessity."

The oars were attached to a crank shaft that when operated in a back-and-forth motion by the crewman inside resulted in a back-and-forth motion by the oar blade on the outside of the hull. This oar blade was hinged in the center, vertically, in such a manner that it would fold like a book on the forward motion and open like a book on the backward motion. This motion and folding were, like some have noted, like a duck's foot in swimming.

It was noted in building a model of one oar station that the designer's concept of rotating the oar 180 degrees would allow the "backing" of the oar motion and reverse the thrust was in error, there was insufficient room for that motion on the inside of the boat.

Re-fitted Propulsion:
The propulsion system was changed starting in August 1862 at the Washington Navy Yard by Martin Thomas and a crew he brought from Philadelphia. The screw propeller was cast in Philadelphia and is assumed to be a four bladed screw of a design similar to that used in Hunley and that shown illustration of the USS Monitor. This design indicated the propeller to be about 4 feet in diameter.

The hand crank system for the screw propeller would have to be offset from the internal centerline of the hull to clear the ballast chamber and emergency release weight tubes. The crewmen who operated the crank would sit sideways in the hull similar to the Hunley arrangement.

Weapons:
The primary weapon carried by the Alligator was a diver and one or more limpet mines he carried and attached to or left in the vicinity of a target. In addition, the diver himself could fulfill missions that involved removal of neutralization of enemy obstacles such as mines. The auger De Villeroi shows in the drawings is not mentioned in any of the written descriptions, therefore it is assumed that it was not installed.

It has been conjectured by the group that there is a possibility that the Alligator may have been equipped with a spar torpedo or a towed mine if it had made it to Port Royal and been assigned to attack targets such as the Confederate ironclads in Charleston.

Color:
De Villeroi stated in a letter that he painted the boat green on the outside and white on the inside. The green was to make the boat less visible underwater, and the white was to enhance lightness inside for habitability. This concept of making the boat less visible by painting it green is the first known discussion of the practice of camouflage coloration of a U.S. submarine.

SUMMARY OF ALLIGATOR SPECIFICATIONS	
COLOR:	GREEN
DESIGNER:	BRUTUS DE VILLEROI (1794-1874)
BUILDER:	NEAFIE & LEVY, PHILADELPHIA NAVY YARD
LAUNCHED:	MAY 1, 1862
LENGTH:	47 FT.
BEAM:	4 FT. 8 INCHES
HEIGHT:	5 FT. 6 INCHES
PROPULSION:	OARS; SCREW PROPELLER
FEATURES:	AIR PURIFYING SYSTEM, DIVER LOCKOUT CHAMBER
COMMANDER:	SAMUEL EAKINS
CREW:	22 WITH OARS; 8 WITH SCREW PROPELLER
FIRST MISSION:	JUNE 25, 1862, DESTROY BRIDGE OBSTRUCTION
LOST:	APRIL 2, 1863, IN WATERS OFF CAPE HATTERAS

Appendix F
Correspondence Documenting Lincoln's Visit to the USS *Alligator*

Re: Lincoln visiting Alligator:

5-Mar-1863
CITATION: NARA RG71, Misc. Ltrs. Sent and Recd, Bureau of Yards and Docks 1861-1863, Schott, G.B. to Smith, Joseph, 2/27/1863
From: Schott, G.B/Thomas, Martin
To: Smith, Joseph
Dated: 2/27/1863
SFLM Doc#143
Transcript

Dear Sir

Yours of the 26th came to hand this morning and I was much astonished and grieved at the tenor of it. I thought you understand all the conditions and the Contract for the Boat. It was continued between Capt. Davis and Mr. Hirst to stand as originally made; Six Thousand Dollars to be paid on acct., Balance when tested. Since then, you have paid $2000 more on acct which has all and a great deal more been expended. You will not forget that I was always in doubt as to her speed by the oars and I told you so. However, she was sent to James River; I followed as a volunteer at my own expense; Capt. J. Rodgers would not risk our going up to remove the obstructions but ordered her to

Fortress Monroe from whence she was ordered to Washington. Lieut. Selfridge was placed in charge; he objected to her want of sufficient speed and requested a survey by an Engineer. Mr. Stimers made the examination and reported she could not be made to obtain any considerable speed. I differed with him and after the report was made to Asst Secy Fox, he authorized me to go to Philadelphia and get the machinery for a stern screw propeller and that it should be put in at the Navy Yard Washington. (I thought you knew all about it.) I ordered the machinery, forwarded it by Express, started the workman at it when Commo. Wilks vessels arrived and the men were taken off, and so it happened several times, until at last I sent men from Philadelphia (paying their passage) and paid them additional wages. Finally, the boat was finished and launched and tested as to her speed (the only thing not already obtained). She with twelve green men (instead of drilled crew of ten or twenty) obtained a speed of from five to seven knots an hour, nearly double what was required. President Lincoln, Mr. Fox and General Butler and Prof Horsford witnessed her performance perfectly satisfied I believe. Prof Horsford descended in her and remained submerged for one hour and seventeen minutes and was perfectly satisfied as to that part. I thought you knew all this. I think I am not claiming anything but what is fairly and justly due on my account. I have had more work and worriment with this Boat than with all the other business of my life. I have been sick nearly all the time wince we left James River, although I have been frequently in Washington attending to and hurrying the work; and for the last ten weeks I have been ill at home and cannot leave the house with disease of the lungs, or I would have seen you in person of writing. I am sorry to trouble you with so long a letter but cannot explain fully in fewer words. I regard the Boat now as the greatest success. She can be made to do anything and still remains at the Navy Yard Washington.

S/
Martin Thomas
Dictated to G.B. Schott.

ACKNOWLEDGMENTS

I am indebted to all of the individuals — in the U.S. Navy, NOAA, elsewhere in government, academia, museums, and the maritime archeological community — who endeavored to rediscover a "mysterious submarine," the USS *Alligator*, and, ultimately, who went to sea to attempt the impossible: to find it. They are naval officers, scientists, historians, archeologists, educators, students, and enthusiasts. I learned a great deal from them, and without them there would be no story to tell.

In writing this book, I am also indebted to the individuals who graciously worked with me along the way, and without whom I could never have undertaken this project — never mind write the book. The first is Jay Cohen, formerly RADM Cohen, and his wife Nancy. They proposed that I tell the story of re-discovering the USS *Alligator*. They encouraged me when I had doubts, helped me remember people and events, read early draft materials, and reviewed the completed manuscript. David Hall also encouraged me to write this story and then dug deep into his personal files, generously giving me everything he had on the *Alligator*. He reviewed early drafts and the completed manuscript and directed me to other participants who would be of help.

Tony Reyer reviewed the manuscript, and from the very beginning of the process, he shared his *Alligator* project notes as well as Mike Overfield's. Tony had the foresight to squirrel away many of Mike's original notes, even his future plans to continue searching for the *Alligator*. These notes were vital to filling gaps in the story. Dave Clark, the consummate filmmaker, read early drafts and encouraged me. Most importantly, he provided me with everything he had amassed during the project and thoughtfully steered me through events. He, too, reviewed the final manuscript. Jim Delgado, who came to work with me at NOAA just as the *Alligator* project was winding down, reviewed early draft materials and encouraged me to complete the story. Jim is one of the most prolific marine archeologists on the scene today, and his review of the final manuscript was insightful. A mentor and collaborator, Steve Burns, reviewed parts of the manuscript and, as usual, he gave me sound guidance.

I am especially indebted to Jim Christley. He wrote the original *Civil War Times Illustrated* article, which Nancy Cohen read, starting it all. He was truly invaluable to my "getting it right" with this book. Jim provided me with every note, letter, and piece of information he uncovered from the very beginning — when he first came across a reference to a "Submarine Propeller" — as well as everything he discovered during the project. Using his creative mind and artistic talents, he produced a unique body of historic art as he painted images of the *Alligator* as he envisioned it. With his permission, I have used many of these illustrations throughout the book, including the cover. Lastly, he shared his deep technical knowledge of the *Alligator* and his theories on how it must have worked. I don't think there is anyone since the time of Brutus de Villeroi who knew more about the workings of the *Alligator*. I told him it was a good thing he hadn't sent me his material until I was well into the first draft. Otherwise, I might have been so overwhelmed I wouldn't have written this book at all. There might be a lesson in that.

I am indebted to Ann Boese, my editor, who has accompanied me from the beginning of my writing journey. This book is our fourth project together. She always makes me look better than I am, and I am always learning from her. Certainly, my readers have benefited from her skills and talent.

Lastly, I am indebted to my wife Arlene. She indulges me wherever I plop down to write and also allows me to bore her with my ideas for a passage I am thinking about or writing. She always tells it to me "like it is." I could never have had the adventures that led up to the *Alligator* saga, as well as so many other experiences, without her support. The people who support us in life are even more important than those who accompany us on the adventure. I have been very lucky.

About Atmosphere Press

Founded in 2015, Atmosphere Press was built on the principles of Honesty, Transparency, Professionalism, Kindness, and Making Your Book Awesome. As an ethical and author-friendly hybrid press, we stay true to that founding mission today.

If you're a reader, enter our giveaway for a free book here:

SCAN TO ENTER
BOOK GIVEAWAY

If you're a writer, submit your manuscript for consideration here:

SCAN TO SUBMIT
MANUSCRIPT

And always feel free to visit Atmosphere Press and our authors online at atmospherepress.com. See you there soon!

About the Author

DANIEL J. BASTA was the Director of the Office of National Marine Sanctuaries in the National Oceanic and Atmospheric Administration (NOAA), within the U.S. Department of Commerce, from 1999 to 2016 when he retired after 37 years of government service. His extensive experience with joint U.S. Navy history projects included those involving the wrecks of the USS *Monitor*, the USS *Conestoga*, and others. He was a member of the Senior Executive Service (SES) for more than two decades and had an extraordinary career both inside and outside of government. He is well known as an explorer, adventurer, and master diver who has traveled the world. Since retirement, he has become a writer and author, spinning the tales of his adventures, sometimes to the wildest of places, and the colorful people he finds there. What makes his books and short stories compelling is that they are always about people, always true, and always convey useful lessons to everyone who reads them. This is his third book.

www.ingramcontent.com/pod-product-compliance
Lightning Source LLC
LaVergne TN
LVHW041951070526
838199LV00051BA/2981